Early Explorations in Science

Second Edition

Exploring Primary Science and Technology

Series Editor: Brian Woolnough
Department of Educational Studies, University of Oxford

Science is one of the most exciting and challenging subjects within the National Curriculum. This innovative new series is designed to help primary school teachers to cope with the curriculum demands by offering a range of stimulating and accessible texts grounded in the very best of primary practice. Each book is written by an experienced practitioner and seeks to inspire and encourage while at the same time acknowledging the realities of classroom life.

Current and forthcoming titles

Jenny Frost: *Creativity in primary science*
Jane Johnston: *Early explorations in science*
Anne Quatter: *Differentiated primary science*

Early Explorations in Science

Second Edition

JANE JOHNSTON

OPEN UNIVERSITY PRESS

Open University Press
McGraw-Hill Education
McGraw-Hill House
Shoppenhangers Road
Maidenhead
Berkshire
England
SL6 2QL

email: enquiries@openup.co.uk
world wide web@ www.openup.co.uk

and Two Penn Plaza, New York, NY 10121-2289, USA

First published 2005

A catalogue record of this book is available from the British Library

ISBN-13 978 0335214723
ISBN-10 033521213472
Library of Congress Cataloging-in-Publication Data
CIP data applied for

Typeset by BookEns Ltd., Royston, Herts.
Printed in Poland, EU by OZGraf. S.A.
www.polskabook.pl

For Montague Doggett. Thank you

Contents

List of figures, pictures and tables

Figures

Pictures

Tables

Acknowledgements

I would like to acknowledge a large number of people who have informed my practice, supported my reflection and helped me in my research,

- colleagues past and present in school and higher education for showing me alternative perspectives;
- practitioners who have kindly given me opportunities to try out ideas and observe their practice;
- students who have endured (and hopefully benefited) from our interactions and have given me new insights into pedagogical development;
- the many children who continually renew my enthusiasm for teaching and science;
- schools who have allowed me to take and use data and photographs of practice in action;
- Chris, Emily and Andrew for continuing to help, hinder and encourage.

1

Early-years science experiences

In the early years children develop rapidly, physically, socially, emotionally, cognitively and linguistically. Their scientific development results from the physical and social experiences they encounter and their personal exploration. It is dependent on the development of language and is affected by (and itself affects) the other areas of development. From the moment of birth, or even from the moment of conception, children are developing scientific ideas about the world around them. In the womb the foetus develops not only physically, but emotionally and cognitively; being able to make use of many senses, for example, recognizing and being comforted by a variety of sounds. A baby soon learns to recognize voices, music and other familiar sounds and will turn its head towards its mother's voice or settle to a familiar melody.

As they grow, babies learn quickly about the world around them. They learn about the existence and effects of gravity, as they drop things out of their prams or high chairs and it becomes a game to throw away your toys and wait for someone else to rescue them. These young children know exactly where to look for discarded toys: they look down. Through experience they have learnt a theory about the world around them, that when you drop things they fall. At bath time the concept of forces is established further through exploration of floating and sinking. Bath toys can be pushed under the water and some will bob back up, while others will sink. Other toys can be made to sink by filling with water. Children spend countless hours filling containers and emptying them, siphoning water through tubes, splashing and 'swimming' in the bath. Bath time is a wonderful opportunity to explore many scientific phenomena in an everyday setting. Bubble bath, shampoo and soap all provide opportunities to explore materials and how they change. A bar of soap can be explored in a number of ways, squashing, making bubbles, soap shapes or mixing soap and water. Thus playing in the bath is quite likely to result in a liquid soap mess, but will also lead to some understanding of the nature of materials and what happens when you mix them.

Early meals will also establish ideas about the nature of different materials, the mixing of materials and how those materials change. Children soon learn that rusks are hard but ease growing teeth, whereas liquidized food is sloppy and soft. When food is given separately it is great fun to mix it all together to form a mess, even if you are not going to eat it. Spoons make nice noises on the table and attract attention, and drinks will spill out if held upside down, even in teacher beakers.

Children's toys will help to establish ideas and skills in science. Children will explore their toys, or even the boxes they come in! They learn to look closely at the toys and explore how they work. They will often find new and novel ways of playing with their toys, but all are valid and will help to develop their ideas and skills. Mechanical, electrical and magnetic toys begin to develop ideas about energy and movement, as well as other types of energy such as light, sound and electricity. Noisy and musical toys develop ideas about sound. Construction toys develop ideas about structures and forces. Cycles, swings, climbing frames and other large toys develop knowledge about balance and movement. Through all the normal exploration of childhood, children will be developing many scientific concepts, but they will also be developing scientific skills. Hand-eye co-ordination, fine motor skills, observational skills, classification skills and prediction skills will be of use in later scientific development. Walks in the woods, or in the local park, visits to adventure playgrounds and interactive museums, bus and train journeys and holidays will all add to these experiences and widen the developing ideas, skills and attitudes. Children will learn about the seasons, flowers, animals, trees, the weather and much more. The birth of new brothers, sisters, cousins or friends will provide knowledge of pregnancy, birth and growth. Personal hygiene and cleanliness, sickness and daily routine will help to develop skills and knowledge which will be of use in later life.

Throughout the early years of life scientific concepts, knowledge and skills are being developed through exploration of the child's world. Children's physical, emotional, cognitive, social and language development will all affect the quality of their early explorations.

Figure 1.1   Factors affecting the quality of early explorations

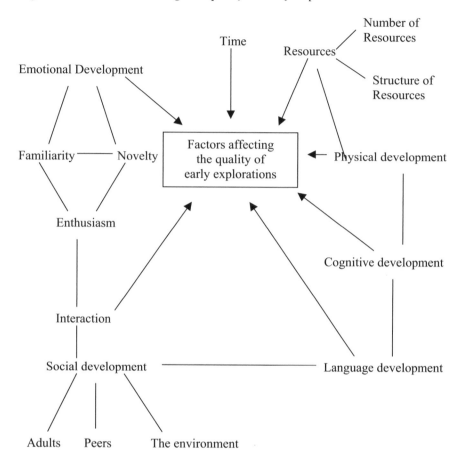

Physically, children should be allowed and encouraged to interact with their environment and explore scientific phenomena in their world. The importance of experiential learning was first identified by Rousseau (see Rousseau, 1911). He advocated a form of child-centred learning where the learning environment should accommodate the child rather than be accommodated by the child. The more child-centred, exploratory experiences children have, the greater their scientific development is likely to be. Providing a variety of different exploratory play resources will assist this development. Children should be encouraged to explore as many diverse resources as possible and should only be restricted by a concern for safety and consideration of other living things. Care should be taken that gender bias is not exercised, even unintentionally, and it is important not to discourage children in their experiences. Children who are discouraged from construction toys will be denied important manipulative and structural experiences; as children discouraged from 'dressing up' will have fewer opportunities to explore different textiles and their properties. Children's physical development will also affect their ability to explore the world around them. Brain development, gross and fine motor development and health will all have an effect on young children's ideas, skills and attitudes about the world around them. The link between physical development and learning was a primary focus of the work undertaken by the McMillan sisters, Rachel and Margaret, in the early part of the twentieth century. They identified the importance of health and diet for learning and cognitive development (see McMillan, 1930).

It is also important to provide ample time for exploration to occur. Children need time for free exploration and should not be rushed from one experience to another. We all value a period of quiet contemplation in our lives, and children are no exception. If we rush them from one experience to another they will have little opportunity to try out their developing ideas and build upon existing ones. At this young age much learning occurs through trial and error, and this takes time and patience. Strangely enough, children appear to have more patience at this age than we give them credit for and will explore a simple toy for a considerable length of time. As children develop, their interest appears to be held for shorter periods of time, perhaps because we teach them to 'value' time!

Emotional development and affective factors will also affect the quality of early explorations. The importance of emotional development on other aspects of child development has long been recognized (Erikson, 1950; Maslow, 1968; Bowlby, 1969) and there is evidence that stable childcare and adult interaction in the early years positively affects both emotional, social and cognitive development (Field, 1991; Siraj-Blatchford *et al.*, 2002). Children who have a larger number of carers in the early years are more likely to be less emotionally stable and seek out familiar experiences. Children will benefit from both new experiences and returning to old ones. They need to return to familiar play resources and see different ways of exploring them, and this sometimes occurs best if access to play resources is restricted. Toys put away for a few weeks are like new toys to the young child and can stimulate new exploration. Structuring playtime can help to prevent children from sensory overload through having too many toys or play resources, or from moving quickly from one activity to another. If children are used to having all their toys out at the beginning of every day then they will quickly become bored with them. If different combinations of toys are provided they may find new and novel ways of exploring them.

Table 1.1 Theorists and their influence on our understandings of early scientific development

---

J. J. Rousseau (1712–78)
Rousseau has been called the 'Father of Education' and his philosophy led to the pedagogy of practical development in the early years (experiential learning). Rousseau realized that children had a different way of thinking to adults. He convinced educators that education should be child-centred, with expression rather than repression being central (Rousseau, 1911).

F. Froebel (1782–1852)
Froebel (1826) developed ideas for the education of pre-school children, aged between three and seven years. He founded the first school for pre-school children, which he called 'kindergarten' (children's garden). He stressed the natural growth of children through action or play.

J. Dewey (1859–1952)
Dewey developed educational principles that emphasized learning through varied activities rather than formal curricula. He opposed authoritarian methods of education, that is the training of children (or keeping them occupied), which he felt did not prepare for a democratic life, although he did advocate guidance (Dewey, 1916). He began a shift from school-centred education towards more child-centred education.

R. McMillan (1856–1917)
M. McMillan (1864–1931)
Both Rachel and Margaret McMillan (1911) recognized the importance of the health of the child as well as the mind of the child. They understood that education is more effective when children are well fed and clothed. Their work led to free school meals and milk for the most deprived children in our society.

R. Steiner (1861–1925)
Steiner's philosophy is one that advocates the importance of spiritual growth and holistic education. He identified the importance of children engaging with the natural world. He believed that children should not be forced into formal learning at an early age and that education involves developing purpose and direction (Steiner, 1996).

J. Piaget (1896–1980)
Piaget (1929) identified stages of cognitive development which have helped us to understand the way a child thinks. He stressed the importance of young children's practical experiences in determining their understandings. His theories have influenced the way we teach and the concrete experiences we offer young children.

L. S. Vygotsky (1896–1934)
Vygotsky (1962), believed there was a strong interrelationship between language and thought. He identified the importance of interaction by skilled

adults in cognitive development; zone of proximinal development (Vygotsky & Cole, 1978).

E. Erikson (1902–94)

Erikson (1950) identified the importance of a loving and emotionally stable home life on the emotional development of the child and motivation to learn. He formulated theories on the influence of culture and society on child development and identified how conflict resolutions can be supported by carers.

A. H. Maslow (1908–70)

Maslow identified a hierarchy of needs, whereby each level needs to be fully met in order for development at the next. Physiological needs are at the base of the hierarchy, with safety next, followed by emotional and esteem needs. Each level needs to be met in order to achieve self-actualization. Significant problems in one area of development during childhood can result in lack of development (Maslow, 1968).

B. D. Plowden (1910–2000)

Plowden, chair of the National Committee on Primary Education. Her report (DES, 1967) advocated a child-centred approach, whereby *'initial curiosity, often stimulated by the environment the teacher provides, leads to questions and to a consideration of what questions it is sensible to ask and how to find the answers'* (DES, 1967: 242). She also recognized the importance of parental partnership in early education and the idea of 'learning readiness'.

D. P. Weikart (1931–2003)

Weikart developed a co-ordinated set of ideas and practices in early childhood education based on Piaget's theories of development. The High/Scope curriculum is underpinned by the belief that children are active learners who learn best from activities planned and executed by themselves (Hohmann and Weikart, 2002).

I am concerned that current concerns in the UK about child protection may adversely affect children's emotional development in the early years, the quality of exploration and both cognitive and social development. We appear to take a very different stance on children's emotional development from other cultures (for example, Brazil), which regard emotional development to be as important as cognitive development. Indeed, if we are to develop learning experiences for children that are excellent and enjoyable (DfES, 2003), we need to consider the importance of emotional and social development as factors affecting the quality of exploration. The amount and type of social interaction during exploratory play can support social, emotional and cognitive development. In the early years, the most important interaction occurs with adults. Too little interaction and the children may lack motivation and lose interest quickly. Too much adult involvement and the exploration may be too structured, the children may become too dependent on adult help and opportunities may not be provided for free exploration, negatively affecting development. Through these explorations, children will also be developing useful scientific attitudes. Their explorations can encourage them to be curious and inventive and begin to ask questions about their world. When children are interacting with adults, other children and exploring the world around them, they will also be developing vocabulary and language complementary to social and cognitive development.

Children are constantly learning about the world around them and the scientific phenomena they meet and the scientific concepts they develop are relevant to their world. Early-years children will have some very firm cognitive ideas about the world around them. These ideas are the result of a whole range of experiences, and even though they are sometimes limited in understanding, they can be wide ranging and diverse. When they enter more formal education these experiences, and the ideas developed as a result, will have an important influence on their subsequent cognitive development. Children do not start school devoid of scientific ideas. No one is completely ignorant of science, but some of these early scientific experiences will be of more benefit than others. Children who have had considerable and good quality early-years experiences will benefit in many ways. My own and others' classroom experiences and research (Moyles *et al.*, 2002; Siraj-Blatchford *et al.*, 2002) have indicated that children who have stimulating early-years experiences such as good parental/home/carer interaction, playgroup, crèche and nursery experiences, are likely to be advantaged. Where there is quality interaction, cognitive development can be enhanced and children can exhibit elements of cognitive behaviour and language more advanced than we would expect at their chronological age (Piaget, 1929; Vygotsky, 1962). The experiences of young children may contain abstract ideas about a wide range of scientific phenomena, but the scientific knowledge being developed by the young children will be the result of concrete experiences. In many instances young children will be developing knowledge about scientific phenomena but unaware of its scientific nature. At a later stage of development we will be able to focus attention on the ideas developing from these early experiences and guide understanding. However, we should remember that full understanding of any phenomenon is a long-term goal.

Children's birthdays and schools' admissions policies mean that some children have additional formal early-years experiences. In the UK, children born between 1 September and 31 August of the following year will be in the same academic year and will move through the key stages together. However, school admissions policies differ. All children should begin their period of compulsory schooling by the beginning of the term after which they are five years of age, but they may begin earlier. Some children will begin school at the beginning of the academic year in which they are five years of age, others the term before their birthday and others the day after their birthday. In addition to the quality and quantity of early-years care and education, the differences in school admissions policies and the subsequent length of time in Key Stage 1, there may be differences in both maturation and pre-school experiences. Children will develop differently and at different rates. Increasingly, premature babies are surviving into infancy and adulthood, but they may be less mature than children born at full gestation. All children will have different experiences and respond differently to them. The result of these differences is a wide mix of abilities and experiences within even our first classroom, making the role of the teacher more challenging. For example, children born on 1 September may have stimulating early years (home and playgroup experiences) until they are three years old. They may enter the Foundation Stage and have quality nursery and reception experiences from three years of age, spending three terms as reception infants before moving into Year 1 at the beginning of the academic year in which they are five years of age, when the class size is small. Other children may be born on 31 August of the following year but be in the same academic year. They may have poor early-years experiences, and no nursery education. They could begin school the term after their fifth birthday, immediately entering Year 1 with older children who have had Foundation Stage experience. At the end of Key Stage 1 the result is that some children entering Key Stage 2 have seven full years of stimulating experiences to reflect on, while others have only two years at Key Stage 1 to enhance their development. As educators we can ensure that the two or three years of compulsory education at Key Stage 1 are stimulating and we can provide opportunities for quality exploration, but we have no control over the early-years experiences of many of the children we teach. As a result, children entering school at five years of age may have diverse needs and abilities.

Parents are very important adults in providing quality early-years exploratory experiences for their children. Even after children enter formal education, parents are acknowledged as the prime carers and educators of their children (QCA, 2000). Very few parents set out with the intention of harming their children's development. Most want to provide experiences that will help their children's development in school and beyond. Some are not informed about the benefits of different experiences for different skills and conceptual development. If parents are not aware of the benefits of experiences that can develop fine motor skills, spatial awareness, observational skills, personal skills and language and conceptual development, they will be unable to provide the best opportunities for their children. Being a parent is one of the most difficult jobs in the world and it is the job we are often least prepared for. We should not assume that all parents are aware of the need to provide different experiences for their children any more than we should assume that they are aware of details about birth and pregnancy. Our society provides support during pregnancy, birth and early life and then only interferes if we make a complete muddle of child-rearing. I met one small child in her first year of life who was unable to play with toys, had difficulties feeding and would not handle her food. Her carers knew nothing of the benefits of talking to her and giving her opportunities to handle food and toys, to put things into her mouth and explore what they feel, taste or smell like. When she smiled it was rare and the first 'raspberry' she blew was a milestone. Even at this young age it took considerable efforts to begin to provide the missed opportunities and make up for the lack of early development. However, we must not assume that all parents have less knowledge and experience of development and care than we do. Adults trained in childcare will have great experience of child development, teachers will have knowledge of learning and pedagogical practice, parents will have in-depth knowledge about their child (and maybe other expert knowledge too). The early-years child is thus surrounded by adults who have the knowledge to provide quality care and provision, provided they 'work together in an atmosphere of mutual respect within which children can have security and confidence' (QCA, 2000: 11). It is essential that this partnership works in the best interests of children, utilizing the expertise of all concerned.

Early-years experiences are diverse and numerous; before children arrive in school they experience science in all aspects of their lives. As teachers, we need to be aware of these experiences and their importance in subsequent school development in order effectively to develop scientific ideas, skills and attitudes in the children we teach. It is helpful not only to have an awareness of the types of experience children have, but also to have a clear idea about the nature of our own science experiences. These experiences have helped make us who we are and are important in understanding our own perspective on science. For example, I can remember positive science experiences before and during primary school which have helped to make me feel positive towards science and assisted my early scientific understanding. I have, however, my fair share of horror stories about later science experiences which not only tempered my enthusiasm for a while, but also hindered my development, particularly in physical sciences.

Additional important understanding comes from knowledge of the history and philosophy of science. This is not only of great interest but also of great importance in understanding the relevance of science to individuals and to society. Questions such as 'What were the major influential scientific discoveries?', 'Who made these discoveries?' and 'How have these discoveries affected my everyday life?' are important to ask and to answer. This knowledge is necessary in addition to understanding the diversity of ideas which make up science, as well as understanding the ideas themselves. In short, we need to know about children, about science knowledge and about the nature of science.

So, what is science?

This question is an extremely difficult one to answer accurately, because science is a vast subject and can be perceived in numerous different ways. Our understanding of science is shaped by our experiences, and these in turn are influenced by our educational system and society. Differences in society and educational emphasis have been found to affect educational practice (Ofsted, 2003) views of the world (Kahn, 1999) science and science education (Johnston *et al.*, 1998). In some societies (for example, Finland, Macedonia, Bosnia) primary science has a biological and geographical emphasis, with chemistry, physics and mathematics being taught as secondary sciences. In some of these societies (Bosnia and Macedonia) as well as others such as Japan and Russia, science education is very knowledge based and there is little skill development or application of science knowledge. In the UK our understanding of science education has changed over the years, from skills-based and child-centred to knowledge-based and curriculum-centred. Ten years ago UK primary teachers would, in the main, describe science in terms of the scientific process, with words such as 'experimenting', 'investigating' and 'finding out' (Johnston *et al.*, 1998), interpreting the question 'What do you think science involves?' as 'What do you think school/primary science involves?' More recently, the emphasis appears to be on knowledge as specified within the curriculum and explaining this knowledge to children (Johnston and Ahtee, 2005; Ahtee and Johnston, 2005). It appears that the major influences on ideas about science are recent and significant experiences that result from the emphasis placed in the primary science curriculum or from the implementation of teaching strategies and school science experiences. Adults have had a variety of science experiences and a broader understanding of science than children and so will have more to draw upon when considering what science is. However, they often do not have a full understanding of the breadth of science applications or the extensive nature of science.

Science is also commonly described as a 'body of knowledge' or a 'body of facts' associated with particular disciplines such as biology, physics, chemistry, geology, astronomy, psychology, information and communication technology (ICT), and so on. Underlying these descriptions of science is the assumption that scientific knowledge is certain and unchanging. In reality, of course, we cannot be certain about knowledge and must acknowledge its provisional nature. New discoveries broaden our understanding of the universe, changing the way we think and the way we view the world. In this way, science is better described as a body of theories, with the present theories being tentative in nature and being replaced with new and better theories as our understanding grows. The provisional knowledge that is science is embedded in general notions or concepts associated with the wide-ranging disciplines. Education in England and Wales has identified certain concepts and knowledge that are associated with science (DfEE, 1999). These can be seen in Table 1.2. The concept of plant growth would be embedded in the discipline of biology or Attainment Target 4 (Sc 2), 'Life Processes and Living Things'. The knowledge within that concept appropriate for young children would include some of the requirements for plant growth (light and water), the parts of a flowering plant (leaf, flower, stem, root) and that seeds grow into flowering plants. The concept of force would be embedded in the discipline of physics or Attainment Target 4 (Sc 4), 'Physical Processes', and would involve knowledge about the movement of familiar objects, about different types of forces and their effects and causes (pushing, pulling, moving, slowing, accelerating, changing direction). As children develop physically and intellectually, so does their understanding of scientific concepts and their knowledge becomes deeper and broader. For our youngest children specific knowledge is not identified in the curriculum (QCA, 2000), but children develop knowledge and understanding of the world through exploration of their environment and the scientific phenomena they encounter in everyday life. This knowledge, and the subsequent understandings that children hold about the world around them, are the focus of Chapter 3 of this book. Like scientific concepts and knowledge, scientific skills also develop in breadth and depth through children's informal and formal experiences. Scientific skills are essentially those skills developed during the scientific process and employed to a greater or lesser extent in our everyday lives. We observe the world around us and begin to ask questions about what we see. We group things together (classify) and identify similarities and differences. We make plans, investigate, predict and hypothesize.

We measure, record, interpret and communicate. If we are buying a new car we look closely at a number of models and compare their features and functions. We test-drive cars, perhaps making notes about each one according to the main criteria we have decided upon. Interpretation and reflection allow us to make informed decisions about each car and our final decision is based upon knowledge gained through the use of scientific skills. A number of the scientific skills are encompassed by exploration and these are described in more detail in Chapter 2.

Attitudes are equal in importance to concepts, knowledge and skills. They fall into two categories: attitudes to science and scientific attitudes or those attitudes necessary to be scientific. Scientific attitudes can be further divided into motivational, participatory, practical and reflective attitudes or affective, behavioural and reflective attitudes. Our success or failure in any scientific endeavour is closely associated with our attitudes to and in science and will in turn affect the development of those same attitudes. These are considered in more detail in Chapter 4.

Our understanding of science education as a subject is clearly a result of our perspective. Those of us engaged in working with children under the age of five will consider science development within the key area of Knowledge and Understanding of the World in the Foundation Stage Curriculum (QCA, 2000).

Educational psychologists would consider science development within three domains,

- Cognitive development (knowledge and understanding);
- Conative development (skills);
- Affective development (attitudes).

Those of us working at Key Stage 1 of the National Curriculum would consider the science attainment targets (see Table 1.2). In all cases, the development being categorized is the same – the development of a child.

The scientific concepts, knowledge, skills and attitudes which young children are developing concern their everyday lives and the world around them. Science is not concerned with laboratories, test-tubes and Bunsen burners, but with real life. It is real science, relevant science, albeit in many cases unsophisticated, undeveloped or even not obviously science (tacit science). Children should be developing scientific concepts, knowledge, skills and attitudes equally. It is important that they form good foundations for future conceptual understanding and do not develop alternative conceptions or misconceptions, but it is equally important that they develop skills that will be of general use in their future lives, in and out of school, and that they develop positive scientific attitudes. Without positive attitudes, conceptual and skill development will be impaired, and without scientific skills both future conceptual development and scientific literacy (the application of science in everyday life) will be impaired.

Throughout this book the phrase 'the nature of science' refers to the science relevant to early-years children (zero to eight years of age), and in

Table 1.2   Science at Key Stage 1 of the National Curriculum 2000 (DfEE, 1999) www.nc.uk.net

---

Sc1   Scientific enquiry
Ideas and evidence in science
Investigative skills
- Planning
- Obtaining and presenting evidence
- Considering evidence and evaluating

Sc2   Life processes and living things
Life processes
Humans and other animals
Green plants
Variation and classification
Living things in their environment

Sc3   Materials and their properties
Grouping materials
Changing materials

Sc4   Physical processes
Electricity
Forces and motion
Light and sound

Breadth of study
Teaching and learning through,
- contexts that are familiar and of interest;
- analysis of the part played by science in development;
- a range of sources of information and data including ICT;
- first hand and secondary data and practical work (including investigations).

Communication
Health and safety

---

this introductory chapter I am referring to the science of life from an under-fives perspective. It should be noted that a wider understanding of science and its nature is essential to enable us effectively to facilitate scientific development in young children.

More formal development of scientific ideas and skills and attitudes

When children mix in more formal ways with other children and adults, in mother and toddler groups, playgroups, nurseries and other Foundation

Stage settings, they develop additional skills and build upon the knowledge they have already developed. They also begin to learn to work with others, to co-operate and to share ideas and skills. These life skills are essential to more formal learning, and children who have not begun to develop them by the time they enter school at five may find school an alien environment and experience cultural conflict. If the first few months of formal schooling are spent learning social skills, then the development of concepts, knowledge, skills and attitudes is likely to be affected. Foundation Stage settings should provide a progression in the development of exploration, from informal scientific development from birth, both widening experiences and deepening them and providing an important stepping-stone to Key Stage 1 education. Although science development is embodied within the key area for learning, Knowledge and Understanding of the World, in the Foundation Stage Curriculum, there are opportunities to develop the breadth of science in other key areas.

Table 1.3   Science within the Foundation Stage Curriculum and Early Learning Goals (QCA, 2000)

- Personal and social development;
  Dispositions and attitudes – interest and motivation in scientific phenomema.
  Social development – works well/co-operates with peers and adults.
  Emotional development – awareness of needs of others (humans, plants and animals).
- Communication, language and literacy;
  Language for communication and thinking – describes scientific phenomena and experiences, uses everyday and appropriate scientific vocabulary.
  Reading – uses fictional and non-fictional books relevant to science.
  Writing – annotates drawings, writes scientific words.
- Mathematical development;
  Calculating – uses calculation in scientific explorations.
  Shape space and measures – sorts, recognizes patterns, explores volume, mass, etc. in explorations.
- Knowledge and understanding of the world;
  Explores objects, materials, living things using all senses. Asks questions about why things happen and how things work. Observes similarities, differences, patterns and change.
- Physical development;
  Handles magnifying lenses, appropriate measuring equipment and other scientific equipment.
- Creative development;
  Describes and recreates scientific experiences, objects and events through art, music, dance and role-play.

Throughout the Foundation Stage, children have opportunities to work collaboratively in a variety of exploratory play situations, which develop all six key areas of development. Explorations of materials can occur using everyday nursery play resources. Finger painting and play dough can provide opportunities for children to explore materials using their senses. Cornflour and water mixed provide a lovely medium for using senses and language development. The addition of food colouring can add to the fun. I have used cornflour and water mix, more formally, to help children with shape or letter formation. It is much more fun than writing or drawing and just as beneficial. Sand and water play can have many scientific dimensions. Wet sand and dry sand can be compared for their building qualities, size and mass. Coloured water, water of different temperatures or different volumes of water can be mixed and compared.

Nursery pets can provide opportunities to observe living things and to care for them. Birthdays, new births and starting school can all provide opportunities to develop ideas about human growth and life cycles. Seasonal weather and its effect on plant and animal life can all provide additional opportunities to consider growth in the environment and to care for and respect growing plants. The opportunities are seemingly endless.

Other play resources will develop ideas about forces. Construction toys can be used to explore how tall a structure can be made. Cycles and other moving toys can be pushed and pulled. Water play can involve development of ideas about floating and sinking. During these explorations the interaction of the carer is important. A questioning approach can help children to develop their ideas, for example 'How can we sink this boat?' or 'What do you think is happening?'

Occasional activities can add to everyday science in the classroom. The provision of ice balloons can provoke wonder and provide additional opportunities to explore. I have used ice balloons, initially described by Ovens (1987), in explorations with children of a wide range of ages and in a variety of situations (Johnston, 1998; 2001). An ice balloon is made by carefully filling a balloon with water from a tap. I stress the word 'carefully', as experience has shown me that if the balloon comes off the tap, you and the room get very wet! The resulting balloon looks similar to a water bomb. It can be placed in a freezer and left for a few days to freeze solid. It is better if you put it into a plastic container in the freezer, because if it bursts it does make quite a mess. You can use a variety of different shaped balloons or even try other containers. I have tried a rubber glove and it was received with great interest, although the fingers melt quite quickly. Using food colouring, or paint to colour the water or adding glitter or small objects, adds another dimension to the ice balloon explorations. As well as leaving the balloon to freeze solid, a half-frozen balloon can make an interesting comparison and lead to exploration as to how the water freezes and water crystals are formed. Explorations such as these can aid the development of a number of scientific concepts and skills which are described further in Chapter 2.

Early exploration in action

I have initiated ice balloon exploration in a number of different ways. First, I have placed ice balloons on a table or in a water trough and allowed the children to explore freely. Sometimes, I also add water- and air-filled balloons for comparison. I have also wrapped an ice balloon up in newspaper and passed it around a group of children asking them to describe what they feel.

It's heavy.
Big.
Cold.
It's like a frozen chicken.

Picture 1.1   *Children observing ice balloons*

The balloons always create a great deal of enthusiasm. Some children immediately touch the balloons, while others are more reserved and don't touch them until they have looked at them for some time. On one occasion, they pushed them around the table and were surprised because they were slippery. One child noticed the rubber of the balloon had broken and was peeling away a little. She was amazed that there was ice inside the balloon.

Ice!
It's cold!
Freezing!

Then the children peeled the balloons and looked again. They tried sliding one balloon across the table and had great fun exploring its slippery qualities again. They noted that it was easier to slide without the rubber, but offered no explanation of why this was so. Meanwhile the remaining balloon had stuck fast to the table. One child was convinced that this was because it had a small piece of rubber underneath it. He put another piece of rubber under it but it did not stick, partly because he did not leave it for any length of time! However, he was still convinced that the rubber made it stick. The first balloon remained stuck to the table for some time and took considerable efforts to remove so other explorations could continue!

On another occasion, children began by looking at air, water and ice balloons in the water trough but became very interested in what would happen to the different balloons if we threw them outside in the outdoor play area. The children predicted that the air balloon would be blown away, the water balloon would 'splash' and the ice balloon would explode. They were quite disappointed in the lack of explosion when we carefully threw the ice balloon, but were fascinated by the splat pattern on the floor made by the water balloon. This led to further exploration of different sized water-filled balloons and balloons dropped from different heights. As it was a warm, sunny day, they also became interested in the drying splat.

Once, after a period of further exploration and observation I gave the children some magnifiers to look more closely at the balloon. These were not magnifying glasses but plastic rectangular lenses, and created additional enthusiasm. One child put a magnifier to his eyes and, rocking backwards and forwards, cried 'Oooo! Ooooo! Ooooo!' The world through a magnifier was new and novel and far more exciting than the ice balloon. The other children looked at the balloon carefully and while they did not notice the details that older children will notice (see Chapter 2) they focused on the water now puddling on the table.

It's melting.
Going away.
Getting smaller.

When different balloons are put into water, children have been amazed that all float but in different ways. They are particularly surprised that the ice balloon, which feels very heavy, will float. They have spent some time bobbing the balloons up and down and feeling them pushing against their hands. They have noticed that the ice balloon gets smaller in the water and this has led to further discussion about what was happening to the balloon. They decided it was 'getting smaller' because 'it's in the water'. Strangely, the children who had already acknowledged that the balloon was melting into water and that that was why there was a puddle on the table, now thought differently when the balloon was in water. When asked where the ice balloon was going they said 'into the glass', referring to the plastic of the tank. They were adamant that the ice balloon on the table was melting into water but the ice balloon in the water was melting into glass. I introduced a coloured ice balloon after this idea had been expressed, but this did not influence their idea. The colour was going into the water but the ice was going into the glass. This contrasted with reception and Year 1 children (see Chapter 2) who looked strangely at me when I asked where the ice was going and answered, as if I was daft, 'In the water, of course'.

The development of children's ideas from nursery to reception and Year 1 is interesting and apparently rapid. On entering school, children are likely to be more systematic in their explorations, and their ideas seem less random. In explorations of ice balloons with Reception and Year 1 children, described in Chapter 2, the ideas expressed were more mature and illustrated that even a few months made considerable difference in the conceptual development of young children. They predicted that an ice balloon would melt faster in water than in the air, and that if dropped on to concrete it would smash. They were aware that when melting the ice would turn into water and that this was why the water level in the tank rose.

The final point to note with ice balloon explorations, or any other explorations with Foundation Stage children, is that it is important not to use too much equipment. Children should have the opportunity, and indeed are happy, to explore using their senses, and equipment to enhance their observations or aid their explorations should be used carefully. With ice balloon exploration the ice balloon alone is often enough. Magnifiers can add another dimension but are not always particularly helpful in aiding their observations.

Other explorations stem from collections of resources brought into the classroom. These can be provided by the teacher, or added to by the children. I love collections as a stimulus for exploratory work (see Chapter 2) and find that children can add new avenues of exploration each time they are provided. This can be a collection of materials, which can be explored and described, moving toys, which can be sorted for the different ways they move, or musical instruments, which can be played and sorted according to how they make sounds. Collections could include artefacts from all areas of science, but may seem to be non-scientific in the same way that ice balloons are not obviously scientific. Leaves, wood samples, twigs and plants could develop ideas about the variety of living organisms, as could visits by the children's pets. A collection of bones could lead to similar development (as described later in this chapter). A collection of toys in a toy shop could lead to explorations of different toys, what they do and how they work. A collection of collage material could be explored before being used in art work. The ideas are endless and the development great.

A collection of seeds and plants in a garden centre have provided a stimulating role-play area for early-years children in a nursery and a pre-school class (de Bóo, 2004). On one occasion, they made close observations of the seeds, using magnifiers and a computer microscope (Intel, 2001) plugged into a multimedia projector so they could see the magnified seeds on a large screen. The children noted small details on the seeds and one child took especial interest in the very small seeds, working her way through a large pile. She did not communicate with anyone else but showed great interest and clearly noted small details by the way she moved the seeds and observed them. I have also used a slide projector making slides using old slide binders and overhead acetates. If a small object, such as a leaf skeleton or a sycamore seed is sandwiched between two pieces of acetate and put into a slide binder, they can be projected on to a screen and small details and patterns can be noted. The children then began to describe the seeds according to texture and size, sorting them according to size, making three groups (small, big and very big). They told me where the seeds had come from, although this ranged from the supermarket, shops as well as flowers. They used their previous knowledge in this discussion, telling me they had seen seeds before,

In the garden
In the supermarket
At the shops.

They played in the garden centre, undertaking money transactions using seeds as money, as well as plastic coins. They read the seed packet and identified the names of some seeds and read books about plants

Picture 1.2   *Child observing seeds with a computer microscope*

which were in the garden centre. They planted some seeds in trays and pots and showed understanding of the needs of the seeds and plants, watering them and putting them in a sunny place to grow. I even found seeds growing in strange places a few weeks later! A few children began to keep a seed diary, drawing pictures of their seeds and their growth at different stages of development. Some children even grouped together to tidy up the garden centre so that other children could use it. One child who was sweeping up soil with a broom, suggested to me that I could help and showed me where there was a dustpan and brush. Later when I had not complied, he leant on his broom, looked at me severely and said 'Excuse me! I gave you a job to do', so I set to!

Through this role-play, children had opportunities to develop in all six key areas of development:

- **Personal and social development;**
    Dispositions and attitudes. They showed an interest in the seeds and plants and in finding out more about them.
    Social development. They had opportunities to play and co-operate with other children and adults.

Emotional development. They began to be aware of the needs of the plants and seeds and what would affect their growth.

- **Communication, language and literacy;**

    Language for communication and thinking. They talked to each other and to adults, describing the seeds and naming the parts of the plants (leaf, root, stem).

    Reading. They had opportunities to read books about seeds and read the seed packets.

    Writing. Children labelled their planted seeds and some children made annotated drawings in their seed diaries.

- **Mathematical development;**

    Calculating. They had opportunities for counting in their trans-actions in the garden centre.

    Shape, space and measures. They sorted the seeds according to their own criteria (size).

- **Knowledge and understanding of the world;**

    The children explored the seeds, observing similarities and differences between them.

- **Physical development;**

    The children had opportunities to use magnifying lenses, garden tools, watering cans and brooms.

- **Creative development.**

    The children were being gardeners in a role-play setting.

The scientific development of the child

We have an increasing wealth of knowledge from research to assist us in understanding the development of children and can apply this to support our understanding of the child's developing understanding of the scientific world (see Table 1.1). Our resulting ideas about child development and early education are usually a mixture of our understanding of this research and our own experiences with children. As a teacher, my main concern has been focused on cognitive development and my biggest influence the work of Piaget (1950), but my understanding has been enhanced by the work of Vygotsky (1962) and Ausubel (1968). However, as I have developed my understanding of child development, my view of the influence of other areas of development and theorists on early science learning has grown.

Rousseau (1911), the 'Father of Education' was the first person to advocate experiential learning, a principle taken up by later theorists (Fröbel, 1826) and practitioners in the form of play (DES, 1967) and embedded in early in the Foundation Stage Curriculum (QCA, 2000). It is the main way in which young children develop scientifically. Rousseau also convinced educators that education should be child-centred. We struggle to accept this idea even today, despite its being advocated by Dewey (1916), who began a shift from school-centred education towards more child-centred education. Today we are slowly struggling with mixed messages about what is good education with the messages from theorists and experiences about child-centred education, vying with the messages from imposed structures of educational strategies (DfEE, 1998 and 1999a) and a seemingly curriculum-centred system (Cullingford, 1997; Johnston, 2002). We recognize that children learn best when offered varied activities (Dewey, 1916), taking into account that children have different types of intelligence (Gardner, 1983) and learning needs. We also recognize that educational experiences should prepare children to become citizens in the real world and yet much science teaching appears to be divorced from reality and does not apparently support decision-making in adult life.

We are also aware of the importance of physical (McMillan, 1930), social, emotional (Erikson, 1950) and spiritual (Steiner, 1996) development and the effect on cognition and the development of the whole child. We even implement ideas to promote cognition through physical exercise and brain health (Dennison and Dennison, 1994) and yet we have moved away from healthy school dinners, appalling some European colleagues, and free school milk for all. We appear to have forgotten some of our understandings of children's emotional needs and how they affect learning, in our desire to be politically correct and provide a secure environment in which children can learn. We need to be careful that 'secure' does not become synonymous with 'sterile'. We need to understand a child's needs in order that we can provide the correct environment for them to develop scientifically, but we need to remember that we do not all have the same needs.

Cognitively, Rousseau first identified that children had a different way of thinking to adults. Piaget's stages of cognitive development (Piaget, 1929 and 1950), developed further by Vygotsky (1962) and made accessible to teachers through the work of Donaldson (1978), have been further developed through the work of Rosalind Driver (1983 and Driver *et al.*, 1985) and the Children's Learning in Science (CLIS) 1982–9 and SPACE (Centre for Research in Primary Science and Technology CRIPSAT) 1986–90 projects. Cognitive development is considered in more detail in Chapter 3 of this book, but here we will look at the acquisition of early scientific ideas.

While working with three- and four-year-old children in a school nursery I was able to analyse their ideas and assign them loosely to three broad categories:

- factual knowledge;
- fictional knowledge or myths;
- inferred knowledge.

Factual knowledge can be acquired through first-hand experience or through secondary sources such as television, films or books. Children can develop factual ideas about animals from very early picture books. *The Very Hungry Caterpillar* (Carle, 1970) can develop factual knowledge about the life cycle of the butterfly. Children's television programmes can add to this information. Practical experience, observing caterpillars and butterflies in the garden at home and in the wider environment, can further develop these ideas. Fictional knowledge is acquired through secondary sources, mainly the media, tales and stories. Since factual information can also be obtained from these sources, it is easy to see why children are sometimes unable to differentiate fact from fiction. *The Very Hungry Caterpillar* contains some fictional ideas about the eating habits of the caterpillar. While exploring the environment with early-years children, I had one child who consistently told me he could 'hear a lion' or had 'found a snake', using his imagination and fictional knowledge in a factual context. Inferred knowledge results from an interaction between children's practical experiences and the existing ideas that they hold. These ideas may be inaccurate and can have a profound influence on further conceptual development.

All these ideas have been illustrated by the early-years children with whom I have worked. On one occasion, nursery children were given a collection of bones to explore. These included skulls from a sheep, a cow, a rat and a human, vertebrae from a horse and a rabbit, a cow's femur, the jaw bone from a dog, a whale's tooth and other assorted teeth in and out of skulls, horns from a sheep, a deer's antler, and a collection of shells of various types. The children freely visited the table where I had placed this collection of bones, and they explored them with great excitement. In their initial observations they expressed their factual knowledge through their comments. In picking up the femur of a cow one child said 'Bones are for dogs', while another said 'Dogs eat bones'. While looking at the collection of shells the children said 'Crabs live in shells' and 'Shells come from the seaside'. Observation of a large cow's horn led to the following dialogue between a group of three children.

> Horns come from animals. (*Putting the horn on the side of his head.*) A cow.
> (*Putting the horn on his nose.*) Rhinoceros! Rhinoceros!
> (*Picking up a deer's antler.*) Reindeer!
> (*Holding a sheep's horn.*) Here's another one.

One child later drew a picture of the deer's antler and asked for it to be annotated with the words 'This is a deer's horn. It's got a straight bit. It goes on your head.' While illustrating their knowledge as to the types of animals possessing horns, this dialogue also demonstrated an early classification skill, in verbally grouping the horns. This was further demonstrated by the children's recognition of teeth, in and out of animal skulls. The teeth were similar in type and shape, the exception being the whale's tooth. However, the children classified the latter as both a tooth and a horn at different times and were quite happy with its dual role. The children also grouped the shells together. Their ability to group things together illustrated the development of a rule or theory about the objects: the various shells and teeth may be different in type, texture and shape but they have features in common which make them recognizably shells or teeth. It seems that classificatory decisions are made on the basis of observations but that contextual clues may be important, as with teeth in the skulls or jaw bones.

Fictional information or myths can become mixed up with factual information. Sometimes this information is acquired through first-hand experiences combined with creativity and imagination, as with the child who informed me that 'You can hear the sea in shells.' Sometimes this

Picture 1.3   *Children sorting bones*

information comes from stories in books and through the media. While exploring the collections of bones, shells and teeth one child, influenced by ghostly stories or picture books such as *Funnybones* (Ahlberg and Ahlberg, 1980), said 'Skeletons come in the night.' Sometimes factual and fictional sources combine to provide accurate knowledge as with the child influenced by the 'Spot' books who drew a picture of the cow's femur and asked me to annotate with the words: 'Spot's bone. You get bones from the country; I've seen one.' Children can also mix fact and fiction when absorbed in role-play situations. On another occasion, children were playing in a pet shop, which was full of stuffed toy pets. They alternated between caring for the pets and playing with them as favourite fictional characters. They also used their prior knowledge about animals' needs and experiences of shopping. I went to the shopkeeper and asked for a small animal that would not eat a great deal of food or need a lot of looking after. After much deliberation, I was given a rabbit (who could be left in its hutch outside with a run) and a mouse (who could live in a cage). I said that I really only wanted one pet, but the child replied, 'Oh it is a special offer; buy one, get one free.'

Picture 1.4 *Playing in the Pet Shop*

In the bone exploration the children illustrated inferred knowledge through the following comments, together with their actions.

(Looking at the jaw of the dog.) This must be its chin.
(Looking at the teeth in the dog's jaw.) It's from a shark.
(Looking at the eye sockets in a skull.) These must be eyes.

One child, without making any comment, put the horns at the side of the skulls and then his own head, while another child commented: 'They go here.'

The conceptual and linguistic development of these children had been fairly rapid. Within four years they had learnt from a variety of experiences about the world around them. They had learnt through experience and, most importantly, the learning had meaning for them. It was relevant to their lives. Donaldson (1978: 121) recognizes the importance of relevance when she says that 'children can show skill as thinkers and language-users to a degree which must compel our respect, so long as they are dealing with "real-life" meaningful situations'.

In providing experiences for children we need to consider how relevant they are to their lives and make the purpose of the learning explicit where possible. An adult (and science educator) once recalled his nursery experiences to me, describing them as 'boring, boring, boring'. He felt that young science experiences were not worthwhile because they were quickly forgotten, but he went on to tell me about his one positive and memorable experience from nursery. Each day he was asked to turn the sand in the sand pit to allow the sun to dry it out. He was told that this was a very important job because otherwise the children would only be able to play in wet, cold sand. He could see the relevance of the job and its importance grew as a result. It was a pity he did not see the science in the activity, but the anecdote really emphasized for me the importance of relevant science exploration. Some children do not need this amount of relevance. They can learn and enjoy experiences for aesthetic reasons, but we need to provide both relevant and aesthetic experiences for young learners to help to develop their full potential.

Children develop their ideas through a variety of experiences throughout their early lives. Piaget's ideas have been extremely influential in developing our understanding of children's learning. Piaget and other psychologists and educational thinkers have informed us about the needs of children in the development of their concepts and this knowledge has enabled us, for the most part, to make informed decisions which aid development and learning. Vygotsky (1962) and Vygotsky and Cole (1968) placed emphasis on the importance of language development in the formation of concepts and this again is a major principle of the Foundation Stage Curriculum.

Learning for young children is a rewarding and enjoyable experience in which they explore, investigate, discover, create, practise, rehearse, repeat, revise and consolidate their developing knowledge, skills, understandings and attitudes. Many of these aspects of learning are brought together effectively through playing and talking. (QCA, 2000: 20)

Through play and communication, children can develop scientific understandings, skills and attitudes. This is particularly the case where play is either unstructured or structured in a way to take advantage of the children's prior knowledge and interests; then the learning is meaningful. Ausubel's (1968) theory of meaningful learning has formed the basis for much recent research into how children learn and the importance of their early ideas as a basis for future conceptual development. In the past few years there has been a rise in interest in children's early scientific development, but there still appears to be a lack of understanding of how early ideas, skills and attitudes emerge and support later development. For example, children's early ideas or skills are not necessarily recognized as emergent concepts and skills because they are not fully developed and do not have all the characteristics of developed ideas and skills. Although most research on early science has focused on older children above the age of eight it has been useful in identifying misconceptions and development trends, which early-years practitioners and researchers have been able to use as a basis for further research. Along with many other teachers I have found the constructivist (Scott, 1987) approach to be most useful in my science teaching, with learners of all ages. In this approach the importance of the teacher knowing children's existing ideas (Ausubel, 1963) for meaningful learning is stressed as is the children's role in developing their own ideas and constructing their own meanings. Learning at any age is not a passive act. There needs to be a willingness to learn, a motivating force and then some kind of commitment to learn. Early explorations are the key to future scientific development, providing interest, motivation and practical experience. These ideas will be developed in more detail in later chapters of this book. Chapter 2 looks at the nature of exploration in some detail. Chapter 3 looks at the emergent ideas of young scientists and how they develop knowledge and understanding of the world. Chapter 4 looks at the development of scientific attitudes and how they affect and are affected by scientific development. Chapter 5 looks at creativity in early-years scientific exploration and in teaching early-years children. Finally, Chapter 6 focuses on the role of the teacher in the exploratory process through creative teaching and provision.

Summary

- Pre-school scientific concepts, skills and attitudes develop rapidly. There are many factors which influence scientific development in young children.
- Pre-school ideas appear to develop as a result of a combination of factual, fictional and inferred knowledge, acquired in a variety of ways.
- The importance of pre-school scientific development should not be underestimated, as it may have a profound effect on future scientific development.
- Our understanding of early years scientific development is based on a combination of different educational and philosophical theories and practice.

2

The importance of exploration

Exploration is an important element in teaching and learning. I believe that exploration plays a vital part in the development of both early-years scientific skills and knowledge and is a prerequisite for more in-depth development of skills and knowledge, especially in children of primary school age.

What do we mean by the word *exploration*? Dictionaries describe it by using such words as *hunt, research, investigation, pursuit, enquiry, chase* and *quest*. Other words such as *discovery, inspiration* and *revelation* stress its creative aspects (Figure 2.1). We can also use the word *play* to describe exploration, as young children will typically explore, discover and find out about the world around them through play, because, as the Foundation Stage Curriculum identifies, 'well-planned play, both indoors and outdoors, is a key way in which young children learn with enjoyment and challenge' (QCA, 2000: 25). The process of exploration is also associated with a lack of any expectation or preconceptions and with experiential learning, which, as I hope to demonstrate, is the most effective way to establish understanding.

The importance of the scientific process was recognized before the implementation of the National Curriculum, with an emphasis on the development of skills by primary science projects and publications such as the Nuffield Foundation Junior Science Project (1964–6) and the Schools Council Science 5/13 Project (1967–74). The National Curriculum (see

Figure 2.1   What is exploration?

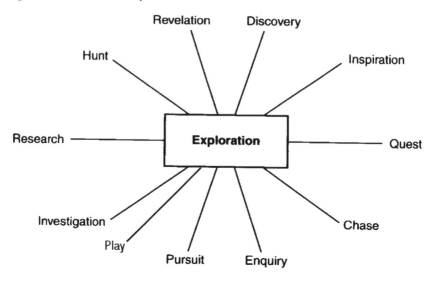

Table 1.2) has endorsed this emphasis on the scientific process and the development of skills since its inception, even recommending in various versions that the skills of science embodied in Sc1 (Scientific Enquiry) should be of equal importance as the content of science embodied in Sc2, Sc3 and Sc4 (Life Process and Living Things, Materials and their Properties and Physical Processes). The introduction of a skills-based curriculum for the Foundation Stage of Learning (QCA, 2000) has further endorsed the importance of basic scientific and generic skills as a basis for future development and learning. In the early-years setting (both within the Foundation Stage and Key Stage 1), this has meant that the development of concepts and knowledge in science should occur as a result of practical experiences. The relationship between the scientific skills involved in exploration and investigation, on the one hand, and scientific conceptual understanding, on the other, can be likened to a double helix, both developing in linked spirals (Figure 2.2). Science therefore needs to be highly practical in order to develop skills and understandings. Children will develop skills if they have the opportunities to practise them through exploration. They will also develop under-standings alongside the scientific skills, for in the words of an old Chinese proverb, 'I hear and I forget, I see and I remember, I do and I understand.'

The development of scientific skills through practical science can take a number of different forms, not all suitable for young children. The most common form of practical science should be explorations, where children

Figure 2.2 The development of scientific conceptual understanding and scientific skills

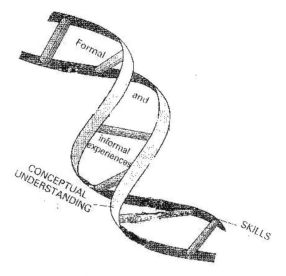

are observing the world around them, asking questions, formulating hypotheses and developing some basic scientific skills. Explorations can be included in the structured play activities that occur in any early-years and Key Stage 1 setting and can be the basis for other types of practical work. They can with older children (from about seven years of age upwards) lead to investigations, where children take increasing responsibility for the work, making decisions about the focus, resources, recording and handling variables involved in a systematic way. Problem-solving science is also suitable for early-years children and throughout the primary school. This type of practical work can be highly motivating and therefore useful in developing scientific attitudes as well as the application of skills and knowledge in a context. Much older children (from Key Stage 3) may also engage in experimentation, a more proscriptive type of practical work, designed to illustrate a concept and promote discussion about the findings. Very occasionally early-years practical science work could involve demonstrations where the activity has safety or organizational implications. Good demonstrations are used sparingly and involve all the children in an interactive way, through questioning, participation and especially interpreting.

The importance of exploration in the scientific process is often unrecognized and yet it appears as a strand in many different learning models in science. Cosgrove and Osborne (1985) provide a useful summary of learning models in science, a number of which involve

Figure 2.3 The scientific process

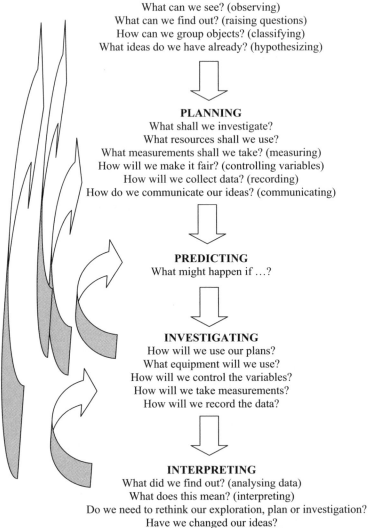

EXPLORING
What can we see? (observing)
What can we find out? (raising questions)
How can we group objects? (classifying)
What ideas do we have already? (hypothesizing)

PLANNING
What shall we investigate?
What resources shall we use?
What measurements shall we take? (measuring)
How will we make it fair? (controlling variables)
How will we collect data? (recording)
How do we communicate our ideas? (communicating)

PREDICTING
What might happen if ...?

INVESTIGATING
How will we use our plans?
What equipment will we use?
How will we control the variables?
How will we take measurements?
How will we record the data?

INTERPRETING
What did we find out? (analysing data)
What does this mean? (interpreting)
Do we need to rethink our exploration, plan or investigation?
Have we changed our ideas?

COMMUNICATING
Can we explain what we did, found out, changed?

exploration, albeit under different guises; Renner's (1982) 'experiences' provided by the teacher, Karplus's (1977) 'exploration' with minimal guidance and Erikson's (1979) 'experimental manoeuvres' are all examples of exploration in science. Cosgrove and Osborne also describe their own model, 'generative learning', which emphasizes exploration as a 'precondition to successful science learning' (Cosgrove and Osborne, 1985: 106), encouraging curiosity and motivating the desire for further enquiry. Within the early years, the Plowden Report (DES, 1967) and the Foundation Curriculum (QCA, 2000) advocate exploratory play for scientific development; a theme reinforced by many (Moyles, 1994; Bennett *et al.*, 1997; Lindon, 2001), as 'it has long been recognized that most high-quality, well-planned and developmentally appropriate experiences in a pre-school setting will have play as the means to promote learning' (Riley, 2003: 19).

Early explorations are often apparently unsystematic and seemingly unproductive, reflecting children's lack of maturity at this stage, but as children mature, there is a development of exploratory skills which enables more skilled exploration and planned investigation to occur. In this way exploration plays a very important part in the scientific process by helping to develop exploratory skills such as observation, classification, raising questions and hypothesizing. These skills are important first steps in the development of other skills in the scientific process, especially planning, predicting and investigating (Figure 2.3). They are additionally important in the development of positive attitudes to science, discussed in Chapter 4.

Observation

Observation is arguably the most important skill in science and certainly the first skill that we develop. One view is that observation is something that children are very good at but that, as they develop, they begin to simplify the world, 'filtering out' things they believe to be unimportant because the world becomes too large for them to observe everything. This filtering out of observations can be seen in many aspects of conceptual development and is an important part of the scientific process, whereby the scientist focuses on those observations of particular relevance to the investigation. As this ability to filter out observations progresses, adults and developing children do not always recognize what they observe. What is important is that we are able to make broad observations before we begin to focus on specific observations. Another view is that observation is a skill which we are very poor in developing effectively and that children's observational skills appear to deteriorate as they develop and they move from unsophisticated general observations to unsophisticated particular observations, rather than improve their skills in both types of observation.

One of the reasons for poor observational development is that our understanding of what observation is and how it develops in young children is not very sophisticated. Observation is more than just seeing (Johnston, 2001); it involves,

- Using all your senses;
- Identifying similarities and differences between objects;
- Observing patterns in objects and phenomena;
- Identifying sequences and events in the world around and in phenomena observed;
- Interpreting observations.

For example, when exploring living things in their local environment, children can listen to sounds around (voices, traffic, birds, the wind). They can smell the natural and man-made smells (cut grass, wet soil, smoke and exhaust fumes, perfume, flowers). They can feel the materials used to make buildings, the texture and patterns of tree bark, the different surfaces under their feet or the sun, rain, wind or cold on their faces. They can see the different colours that make up the green of trees or the red of brick or the brown of bark, look for small animals or evidence of animal life or see the patterns in a leaf skeleton or insects wings. They can feel and see patterns in the habitats of living things and begin to make sense of why plants and animals live in particular locations and what they need to live and grow. They can identify that more evidence of living things can be found at certain times of the year and that living things have similar needs and life cycles. Through this type of exploration, children have the opportunity to develop further skills as a result of their observations; classification of living things, raising questions which can promote further observation or exploration, interpretation of observations and language skills.

Another factor adversely affecting observational development concerns the demands of some modern teaching, which tends to focus on the organization of science activities and the development of knowledge, rather than skills. We seem to be on a treadmill of teaching and learning; we keep running in order to ensure content coverage, while understanding, resulting from quality exploration and investigation, gets left behind and there is little time left for the development of scientific skills. We need to focus on the reality that quality learning is more important than the amount of content covered. Young children are very good observers (Johnston, 2001), especially while interacting, although they can get distracted easily and may need to be refocused (Keogh and Naylor, 2003). As part of explorations, they will, characteristically, make

Picture 2.1   *Children observing in the environment*

use of their senses, notice details, identify similarities and differences between objects and events, put events in the correct sequence and begin to use observational aids (Harlen, 2000). Poor observation has been linked to a lack of curiosity or to over-activity (Harlen, 1977a; 1977b), so that children who, for whatever reason, are withdrawn or overactive do not allow themselves the same opportunities to observe. Early-years children are often very perceptive and creative observers. In observations of ice balloons children have likened the radiating bubbles of air inside the balloons to 'the inside of a peach' and 'hair'. These observations can only be based on the children's previous experiences and, as a result, are obviously limited, but they are also very creative and imaginative observations (Dale Tunnicliffe and Litson, 2002). This creative aspect of children's observations should be encouraged. It is important that we do not impose our own beliefs, which arise from our limited experiences, on children's observations and that we help them to develop confidence in their observations.

Observational skills and creativity can also be seen through children's drawings. For example, when drawing pictures of fish from observation, Rebecca noted the patterns of their scales and made up her own pattern. When drawing a plant, Sarah put it into a decorative pot in her bedroom. In both situations, the detailed observation was not lessened by the creative additions but in fact indicated wider powers of observation. I believe that older children are less able to be creative in their observations and that this is, in part, to do with our teaching. As children develop they learn a great deal about the world around them from hidden messages, from body language and through interpretation. They appear to receive messages about observation in science which devalue creativity and imagination: 'Is your hair really green?', 'Why have you drawn it like this?' The result is that they observe those things they feel we value and they do not often include creative and imaginative ideas or observations.

We can encourage observation in young children by,

- giving them opportunities to observe collections of objects and explore scientific phenomena;
- encouraging children to use all their senses (where safe) in their observations;
- helping children to enhance observations by giving them magnifiers, binocular microscopes, projection screens, stethoscopes, colour charts, etc. as appropriate to their age;
- asking children to describe their observations, giving them new vocabulary as appropriate;
- encouraging children to look for patterns, sequences of events, similarities and differences in their observations;

Picture 2.2　*A child's drawing of a pineapple*

- allowing children to describe the patterns, sequences and interpretations of events they observe;
- asking children questions about their observations;
- allowing children time to draw details of their observations.

Raising questions

The skill of raising questions begins in young children by their asking questions about why things happen and how things work. It then develops into more specific questions about scientific observations and phenomena. As children develop they will begin to identify the difference between productive questions, which can be answered through exploration and investigation, and non-productive questions and use these productive questions and plan how to answer them through exploration and investigation.

Opportunities for explorations and observations can lead to children raising questions. Raising questions is a skill which comes naturally to most young children, and in a learning context the types of question we are attempting to elicit are ones that will promote new explorations and allow investigation. As such, raising questions is central to exploration. It is also a skill closely involved with making judgements about children and assessing their ideas. This is because the questions children raise are likely to indicate gaps in their experience or misconceptions they hold.

However, raising questions is not a skill that appears to develop with age. A visitor to a Foundation Stage or Key Stage 1 setting will be met by a barrage of questions – who? what? how? and, especially, why? In a Year 6 class, despite the development of higher-order skills, questions do not trip readily off the children's tongues. In many ways, the reason for this anomaly lies in the nature of both society and the primary classroom.

As children develop, there can be more sources of information available to them and they do not always need to ask questions to obtain an answer. There are also influences on them which deter them from asking questions. A very important influence is self-image, which is greatly influenced by peer pressure. Asking questions can portray an image that is unacceptable to a child's peers: the child either doesn't know the answer and so is stupid, or wants to know the answer and so is a swot. In a competitive society it is better not to compete than to fail, and in raising questions you definitely cannot win. Children also learn that their questions are often not answered, so that asking questions becomes a pointless exercise. Additionally, asking questions can lead to further work, with teachers using a child's question to stimulate discussion and focus on further exploration or investigation. The only acceptable question for older children is one which distracts the teacher and avoids work. For the teacher, children raising questions can also be a cause for concern, especially in science explorations. The familiar cry of 'What if I don't know the answer myself?' is heard throughout primary classrooms, and it is very hard to persuade teachers that it is both unrealistic and unnecessary to expect them to know all the answers.

In some ways I sympathize with teachers in this situation – we all want to feel secure in our teaching and to provide the best for the children in our classes. Knowledge gives us that security. It is no longer possible to imagine that one person could possess all the knowledge about the multitude of disciplines we call science. Furthermore, it would provide a false picture to children in the classroom if they were led to believe that it was possible for one person to know everything and that their teacher was that person. This, however, is of little practical help in the classroom when faced with a question you cannot answer. In such a situation there are some strategies that I have found useful.

The first is honesty, to admit that you don't really know, or haven't thought about the problem in a particular way. The next strategy is to ask the child for his or her ideas and to begin to explore the issue together. You may not come up with a definite answer but, in doing this, you clearly emphasize a view of the nature of science that is often incompatible with children's views. We need to move away from the view that science is a precise methodology and a body of laws or facts which, if known, logically explain everything. Challenging the children's ideas will help to develop a more realistic view of the nature of science. I choose to encourage the view that science is concerned with developing ideas about the world; the best ideas are the ones you hold until they are challenged by experiences, after which you change, modify or develop them. The child who decided that the ice balloon stuck to the table because a piece of balloon was underneath it (see Chapter 1) developed ideas as a result of experience and needed further experience to challenge these ideas.

Another strategy is to use questioning as a technique to promote exploration and model the questioning behaviours you wish to encourage in the children. Good adult questioning can support children's explorations by encouraging 'thinking skills, language, problem-solving and cooperation' (de Bóo, 2004: 12) and has the additional advantage of showing children that it is fine not to have infinite knowledge. The final strategy is to research the question, either with the child or independently, and return to it later. I was once asked a difficult question about planetary motion by a teacher on an inservice course and, not wishing to give a false answer, I admitted my ignorance and immediately rang the Education Officer at Jodrell Bank, who very kindly gave us an immediate answer. Obviously, this strategy will be less successful if tried with a group of three-, four- or five-year-old children, who will not wait while you find out and whose interest in the answer will be lost quickly anyway. However, further personal research does take you further up the learning curve, and you will be able to answer that question next time! There are a number of informed bodies and associations which can help you in answering those tricky questions. Education officers at science centres, science institutes and professional associations such as the Association for Science Education can all be of help.

The key to developing the skill of raising questions is to provide an atmosphere in your classroom where children feel able to practise that skill, without fear of ridicule or comment. In such an atmosphere you can then encourage children to examine their questions in order to see if they can be answered by further exploration, investigation or research, which of course develops other skills in the scientific process. This can be achieved through:

- the provision of motivating, new and different experiences or different ways of viewing familiar phenomena;
- motivating interactive displays and question tables: for younger children the displays and artefacts themselves support oral questioning. For older children, questions can be written on cards, on tables or on pull-up cards on the walls. Children can be encouraged to interact with the artefacts and questions and try to find some answers which they can share with others. This will also help them to develop respect for the ideas of others;
- the use of a flip chart during initial explorations for writing questions: children's questions can be written on the chart with large felt-tip pens, their questions can be discussed later and decisions as to which questions are productive and can be answered and what to explore further can be made;
- pegging children's questions to washing lines across the classroom to provide a more questioning atmosphere and focus attention on questions raised through observation and exploration: the shapes can represent the subject being explored, so that questions about ice balloons can be written on balloon shapes;
- making question bubbles or speech bubbles with questions raised by children written on them: these can be displayed or brought to a larger group discussion.

Classification

Classification skills can be developed through observation and exploration; such skills are, indeed, necessary before children can effectively investigate further. In order to be able to carry out an investigation successfully children need to be able to see similarities and differences between objects and events and to rearrange them according to features they have in common; in other words, to classify them. Classifying things reduces the number of different impressions children have and allows them to learn from experiences, enabling them to make sense of the world around them. Recognizing the stages in the development of children's classificatory ideas allows us to assist with their learning. At an early stage of their development, children will put objects into groups, but will be unable to give reasons for the groupings that make sense of their actions. These objects 'go together' rather than have a shared feature. They may recognize a feature that distinguishes them but may be unable to communicate this. A further development occurs when children use one feature as a basis for grouping. For example, when exploring a collection of toy vehicles a young child may focus on the red vehicles and will then group all the red vehicles together in one group and then all the other vehicles in another group, regardless of colour. At the next developmental stage children will decide upon a single criterion, such as colour, which differentiates all the vehicles. They will then be able to make several groups, for example, red cars, blue cars, green cars. As children notice that objects can have more than one property at the same time, they become able to classify them and then to reclassify them because of another criterion. Taking cars as an example, criteria could include colour, shape, make, usage, speed and number of passengers. In order to classify objects according to two criteria simultaneously, children need to be able to keep two ideas in mind at the same time. The exploration of a collection of vehicles could lead to investigating the distance travelled by different vehicles down a ramp which is covered with different surfaces. Children who have developed well the skill of classification should be able to identify objects or conditions with a combination of features, without going through the whole classification process.

When children explore collections of objects they have opportunities to classify. When sorting a basket of fruit, linked to the story *Handa's Surprise* (Browne, 1997) Reception children noticed and described simple features of the fruit; colour, shape, size (see also Owens, 2004). They sorted the fruit according to one of the features identified by them. Some children were able to re-sort the fruit using other criteria (either coming from them or suggested by an adult). They described what they could see and feel and drew some of the fruit with attention to detail (see Picture

2.2). During another exploration of a collection of moving toys with Year 1 children, I gave each child a different toy, while they were sitting in a circle. They described them and explored how they worked, before moving to small-group work involving playing, sorting and making simple moving toys. Later, we reconvened the circle and I asked the children to put all the spinning toys in a sorting hoop. The children then chose criteria for sorting the other toys; magnetic, bouncy or push toys. One toy was both magnetic and spun and so the children made three suggestions as to how to sort them:

1. put part of the toy in each sorting hoop;
2. put the spinning part in one hoop and the metal part (the toy was in two parts) in the other hoop;
3. make a new category of spinning and magnetic toys, by overlapping the hoops.

Picture 2.3 *Children sorting a collection of moving toys*

Handling variables or factors

A well-developed ability to classify is basic to logical thinking, particularly to undertaking investigations in science that involve separating variables or factors. Young children should be provided with opportunities for exploration which enable them to handle simple variables or factors. The most simple explorations involve categoric variables. These allow us clearly to identify variables, usually according to observable features such as colour or shape. For example, in our investigation to see which toy vehicle travels the furthest down a ramp the categorical variables are the shape and colour of the cars. This can lead to consideration of fair testing, where children need to identify the key variables; that is, they must identify what they are changing (the independent variable), in this case the vehicle, and what happens as a result or is affected by the change (the dependent variable), in this case the distance travelled.

These are the variables which define an investigation and their complexity can affect the difficulty of the investigation. A categoric variable, such as the colour or type of car, is the simplest, but variables can be much more complex. If we are interested in the distance travelled by each vehicle (the dependent variable), then we are introducing the difficulty of needing to measure the distance, although the use of non-standard measures in early explorations can alleviate this difficulty. If we choose one car and add 10-gram masses to it to see how that affects the distance travelled, then our dependent variable is more complex (called a discrete variable). Changing the dependent variable again to investigate the speed of each vehicle makes the investigation more complex still, because speed has to be calculated from two measurements, distance and time, and is therefore a derived variable. Simple investigations have a smaller number of additional variables to control. These additional variables, or control variables, need to remain constant throughout in order to make the investigation fair. In our vehicle investigation these would include the height of the ramp, the way the vehicle is released, and the surface over which it travels.

Other investigations may involve not just more complex variables but more than one independent and dependent variable. For example, in an investigation to see how far vehicles of different weights travel down a ramp, the independent variable is the type of vehicle and the dependent variable is the distance travelled. If, however, the investigation is changed slightly and the weight of each vehicle and the height of the ramp are considered to see how they make a difference to the distance travelled, then there are two independent variables, vehicle weight and ramp height. Thus the investigation becomes more complex. In another variation, the vehicle weight may be the independent variable but there may be two dependent variables such as distance and time, and these can be calculated to discover the speed of each vehicle, making a third derived dependent variable.

In a typical investigation at this level, Year 1 and 2 children decided to find out whose hands were the largest. They decided to use a tub of marbles and see how many marbles they could pick up. Each child used one hand to pick up the marbles and the number of marbles picked up was counted and recorded. In this investigation the independent variable was the hand used to pick up the marbles. The dependent variable was the number of marbles picked up. In order to make this investigation fair a number of other variables needed to be controlled. These control variables included the tub of marbles, which needed to remain constant for each child, and the way the children picked up the marbles, whether they scooped them up (with the palm of the hand up) or grabbed them (with the palm of the hand down). In this investigation the variables concerned were simple and there was one independent and one dependent variable.

Obviously for young children we do not want a complex investigation with a large number of variables to control. Young children will need to begin with simple investigations with few and simple variables, and the complexity should increase with their ability to recognize and handle variables. This does not mean that a vehicle investigation is too complex for young children, but rather that we need to plan carefully for the investigation and ensure that children are not frustrated by the complexity of the variables. Goldsworthy and Feasey (1997) identify the progression in handling variables and making investigations fair. From open explorations children observe differences and raise questions. This leads to simple investigations where the teacher controls the variables but allows opportunities to consider whether the test is fair or unfair. 'It was fair because we all did it the same way,' is a familiar statement from young children. Further development allows children to handle some variables in an investigation, but other variables need controlling for the children. Our desired goal is for children to plan and carry out investigations having identified and controlled all the variables whatever their complexity.

Hypothesizing and predicting

Children need to have opportunities to make predictions and to hypothesize about observable scientific phenomena or events. Predicting and hypothesizing are often misunderstood skills and considered to be the same. Prediction is about making sensible guesses about what will happen next or in the future. Initial predictions are unlikely to be correct or to be based on significant evidence, but as children gain more experience about the world around them, they should be able to make informed, sensible predictions rather than uninformed guesses. Children are unlikely to see incorrect predictions as valid and will try to change them so they are 'correct'. As children develop and move out of the early years it is desirable for them to see incorrect predictions as useful evidence to support future correct predictions. Hypothesizing involves the explanation of a scientific event or phenomenon; why something has occurred or why it will occur, and so can involve an element of prediction. Initial hypotheses are unlikely to be scientifically correct and may not be obviously based on evidence or experience. As children develop, they should be able to use limited, everyday evidence in their hypotheses and explain events or phenomena. As they move from the early years and into Key Stage 2, they should be able to use more scientific ideas, evidence or research in their hypotheses.

Through explorations and simple investigations, children begin to develop simple predictions and hypotheses. In explorations of vehicles, all children predicted that the vehicles would go down the ramp but they all had different hypotheses as to why. Carl, aged seven, developed the simple hypothesis that the shape of the vehicle made it go fast: 'The car goes down the ramp because it's triangle shaped.' Katherine, aged five, considered friction when she said the vehicle went down the ramp 'because it slides'; and Gareth, aged six, had some early ideas about gravity when he said that the vehicle went down the ramp 'because the ramp's like a big hill and it's falling down'.

Exploration in the water trough can lead to simple hypotheses about floating and sinking. For many children these hypotheses concern the weight of the object, such as 'It will sink because it's heavy' and 'If you put something really heavy on it, it'll sink.' These ideas develop as a result of previous experiences in school and out. The swimming pool, boat trips and bath time all play an important part in developing these hypotheses. Tracey, who had been on a ship, had developed a hypothesis that heavy things floated because of the depth of the water. Jon had noticed that a swimming float 'pushed' against his hand and he thought it might be the 'water pushing'. Floating and sinking was the focus of the first reported year of Standard Assessment Tasks for seven-year-old children in 1990. My son, Andrew, was involved in these, and as they were very practical assessments they provided ample opportunity for children to express their ideas gained through previous explorations and investigations. Andrew came home from school extremely excited about the floating and sinking activities. He had been asked to predict which objects, from a range supplied, would float or sink.

I had to say what things would float and what would sink ... I thought that all the heavy things would sink and all the light things would float. I had a shell that weighed 5 grams and a cork that weighed 55 grams and I thought the shell would float and the cork would sink.

He had not only predicted which object would float or sink, he had offered his hypothesis about floating and sinking: heavy things sink and light things float. He continued: 'But I was wrong! The cork floated and the shell sank, but I think I know why.' He didn't need much encouragement to give me his new hypothesis and his reasoning:

Well, I know an ice balloon is very heavy. [He had made one at home with me.] I could hardly lift it up and it floated in the bucket and I know that a ship is very very heavy and I couldn't pick it up. Well ... I think that when something is light it floats and when it is heavy it sinks but when it gets very heavy it floats again.

Andrew's hypotheses, although not matching the scientific theories, were developed through exploration and investigation. Further practical experience would be needed to try out his new hypothesis about floating and sinking and to provide challenges for it. It is important to remember that a hypothesis does not have to be correct but should 'be reasonable in terms of the evidence available and possible in terms of scientific concepts or principles' (Harlen, 1992: 30). For Andrew, further exploration and investigation was needed to try out his hypothesis and attempt to modify his ideas. This could be done by challenging the children to make something that sinks float and something that floats sink. In water play, I usually include objects such as a ball of plasticine which sinks, but can be made to float by moulding it into a boat shape, marbles (which also sink) can be made to float in the plasticine boat, aluminium foil which floats, but can be made to sink if crushed. I also include a lemon, which floats but will sink if peeled and this particularly challenges the children's hypotheses about floating and sinking, as you have made something which floats smaller and less heavy and it will sink. This occurs because the whole lemon has a lower density (because of the pith) than the flesh of the lemon.

Communication

Exploration can provide a forum for children to develop their ideas about science as well as in science and can provide opportunities to communicate these ideas. Communication is a very important skill to develop in young children (Barnes, 1976; QCA, 2000). In science, Harlen

(1985: 39) describes communication as 'an outward extension of thought', helping to sort out 'what we think and understand' (2000: 41). Early-years children will not record their work in formal ways and so communication becomes an important end point in explorations. It is essential that children are given time to think about their explorations and are given opportunities to express their ideas. This enables them to sort out any muddled thinking: to clarify their ideas and reach a better understanding. Children need to clarify their ideas in order to communicate them to others, and communication often encourages them to evaluate their ideas. Often, we undertake scientific activities with children but forget to think carefully about the ideas being developed. The pressures of the busy classroom seem to dictate that we move on quickly to the next set of ideas and the children's ideas remain half-formed or muddled. Communicating these ideas will help children to be clearer about them. Communication also gives children access to the ideas of others. These, too, may be partially formed and they may conflict with ideas already held, but it is important that children learn to consider their own ideas as tentative and subject to change and this is often the first occasion when this can occur. They may agree with the ideas expressed, they may disagree, but it is important that they think about how they match with their own ideas. If the ideas expressed by others challenge their own beliefs they may feel confused and unhappy and need to undertake a period of further exploration and investigation. In many scientific explorations this communication consists of the general talking that is associated with any classroom activity – the classroom buzz. This is constructive talk where children bounce ideas off each other, express and clarify their ideas, and in the process reach a deeper understanding. A quiet environment is often not the best environment for learning to occur. Not only is it important to communicate with other children, it is also important to communicate with adults who can challenge, encourage and support further exploration and learning. The role of the teacher in facilitating this communication is therefore of great importance. In the Foundation Stage, this type of communication is common and there will be little gained from more formal means of communication or longer periods of large-group communication.

With Key Stage 1 children, situations need to be provided where children can discuss their ideas. This may involve the whole class or a small group of children. The advantage of small groups is that children can all be involved in a meaningful way and are less likely to feel intimidated by the more dominant members of the group. The advantage of a larger group is that there are more ideas to challenge the children and promote discussion, although situations where all children take turns in expressing their ideas can be time-consuming and de-motivating for children. Remember also that early-years children are unlikely to be focused for more than ten minutes on any one task and so it is unreasonable to expect them to sit for long periods of time listening. It is more important for children to engage in quality listening for a short time, rather than for each child to have a turn. As Harlen (1992: 105) has said, if communication 'is mainly a social event, with the emphasis on the opportunity to speak and little feedback in relation to the content, then it may become something of a ritual'. I have asked young children to describe an object (as in the toy exploration above) to another child or a small group of children and then ask one or two children to communicate this to the whole group or class.

Plenary times can provide the occasion for children to review their work and ideas and think about new explorations and investigations, but should not be used routinely to repeat information or show completed work, unless this supports the achievement of the learning objectives. Since the introduction of the literacy and numeracy strategies (DfEE, 1998 and 1999), plenary sessions appear to be a compulsory part of each and every lesson and often they appear to serve little purpose. It is important that they are used in a variety of ways (or not at all), to ensure variety of delivery but also to support the achievement of the learning objectives. I have sometimes used plenary time in a developmental rather than informative way by organizing explorations to develop from the ideas arising from others. Groups of children are given the opportunity to explore a collection of materials over the course of a week. At one time this type of activity would be organized so that, after a brief introduction to the whole class, at the beginning of the week, each group starts afresh and looks at the materials as if for the first time. By the time the final group of children undertake the activity, they have been aware of the resources and the other children's interactions, albeit on an informal classroom observational basis. Sometimes, there was time to discuss findings with each group. Occasionally, a plenary session would take place at the end of the week and the findings of all discussed, although for some young children this is too distant for them to be able to participate fully. More recently, the lesson would begin with a whole class introduction, followed by either individual or group practical work or a demonstration, neither of which will support quality development and interaction, and would finish with a plenary. While there is nothing wrong with these approaches in some situations, an alternative method of organization can be motivating, leading to greater development of knowledge skills and attitudes, and this can be facilitated through better communication. Using the plenary time effectively as an introduction, the activity to explore the collection of materials and to make observations and raise questions about them can be introduced. The first group of children can then communicate their observations and ideas about the materials in a subsequent plenary. All the children in the class can then be encouraged to look for interesting anomalies or patterns in the ideas expressed and to analyse them. This can lead to a decision as to what questions can be answered during the next group's exploration and may lead to some investigation. Feedback from the second group's exploration can promote new ideas and discussion which in turn can help another group to begin to plan an investigation. As a result all the children are immersed in the work of all, and co-operation and the sharing of ideas take on new meaning. I do not suggest that this is a method of organization that is desirable in every situation or should replace the individual development that should occur when children individually explore, raise questions, investigate, develop hypotheses and commu-nicate their ideas to others.

Goldsworthy and Feasey (1997) indicate that young children do not find analysis of their ideas easy. It therefore becomes important that situations are provided which allow them to communicate their ideas in a supportive atmosphere, not in a situation where the teacher dominates (Elstgeest *et al.*, 1985). This can be done by allowing time, during and at the end of science explorations or investigations, to reflect, interpret and communicate and by encouraging children to share their findings and discuss different interpretations with each other, identifying what they have learnt.

Exploration in action

An open-ended, exploratory activity will provide children with opportunities to pursue avenues of enquiry that are of interest to them and allow them to formulate simple hypotheses about their experiences. In an exploratory activity, children engage in observations, raising questions from their observations which can be explored further or which may involve more systematic investigation. As a result of the exploration, children choose differentiated pathways to follow that are consistent with their needs and abilities. There will be a number of learning outcomes, but in each case the outcome is likely to be relevant to the children's learning needs. A more prescriptive activity will involve all children undertaking an identical or slightly differentiated activity, leading to one learning outcome. This learning outcome may not be consistent with every child's needs and abilities and, as a result, some children may not further develop their knowledge or skills; moreover, there may be an element of disillusion or frustration.

This can be illustrated by the following observation of a group of

Year 2 children who were looking at magnetism. They had embarked on an activity that was designed to develop knowledge about which materials were magnetic and which non-magnetic. It involved the children in testing a range of objects and putting a tick or cross beside a picture on a worksheet. The children quickly engaged in, and completed, the task and were then allowed some time for exploration using the resources provided. One child quickly observed that the magnet worked through the table and very excitedly began to investigate which other materials, and which thicknesses of materials, the magnet worked through. Another child observed through her play that the magnet made a paper clip 'jump off the table' when placed above it. She then went on to observe that 'it didn't do it' when the paper clip was placed on a pair of scissors, but the paper clip could be made to 'stand up'. She hypothesized that it was 'the scissors that made it do it', although she could not explain why. A third child had obviously developed a theory that magnets attract all metal objects and, even though the original activity had challenged this by using a variety of metallic objects, he still clung on to this theory. His ideas were, however, challenged by the exploration because he was unable to ignore those objects that challenged him. He decided that all the metal objects which were not attracted to the magnet must be 'aluma', and it was clear that his experiences had included recycling aluminium drink cans. However, he also felt that 'aluma' was a metal and therefore his observations did not fit his theory. At this point, he became very confused and ready to investigate a range of metallic objects to see which types of metal were attracted to the magnet. This exploratory activity was originally perceived by the student teacher as a 'filler', and she was exceptionally surprised to notice how much quality learning was developed compared to the original planned activity.

Another observation of reception and Year 1 children, who were involved in an investigation of materials, illustrates the importance of exploration before investigation to maximize understanding. The investigation involved the children in using a variety of writing implements (pencil, ballpoint pen, felt-tip pen and wax crayon) and a variety of surfaces (plastic, blotting paper, writing paper and wallpaper) and was structured to help control variables. The children had to stick strips of the material on a prepared worksheet and write their names on them using each type of writing implement. It was a lovely, imaginative way to record an investigation, but some children were unsure of the reason for the activity, and when asked what they were doing responded with 'We are learning to write our names' or 'I don't know'. Other children found the activity difficult because they did not understand the worksheet categories or could not fit their names in the spaces provided.

All children would have benefited from an initial period of exploration, allowing them to try out different writing implements and surfaces and being encouraged to develop hypotheses about the suitability of the surfaces and the implements, before investigating further and recording those investigations.

In a final observation of Foundation Stage children, they were exploring the texture of different materials, lavender play dough (with lavender essence and seeds), cornflour, cornflour and water, finger painting, clay and sand. The children explored the materials using all their senses, made and described observations and communicated their ideas to interacting adults. They talked about the 'scrunchy' cornflour, the 'hard but squelchy' cornflour and water and the 'squidgy' and 'smelly' play dough. Through this activity they began to develop skills of observation and communication, knowledge about materials, vocabulary to describe the materials and enthusiasm for learning (as can be seen from Picture 2.4).

Picture 2.4   *Child exploring the texture of cornflour*

Examples of exploratory activities

Having identified how important exploration is, as a prerequisite to investigation, it would be useful to look at some examples of good explorations – explorations that can lead to good investigations. Explorations with ice balloons are a favourite because the context is not obviously threatening and scientific. Chapter 1 looked at what ice balloons are, how to make them and some of the ideas that pre-school children have about them. I shall now explore the form these explorations can take and the sort of investigations they can lead to.

In explorations with ice balloons children need to have an opportunity to observe the balloon without any other resources. This is because they can be easily influenced by the resources you provide. An ice balloon on a table or in a water trough can promote enormous discussion and other resources can be introduced when the children appear to need them. There is no need to give magnifiers until the children have observed features that need magnification and there is no point in introducing thermometers if the children do not understand standard temperature measures and have not had the opportunity to measure the temperature qualitatively: to feel for themselves. From initial observations, the children will raise questions about the balloon, some of which can be further explored or investigated, and it is at this point that other resources can be provided to aid these investigations. With young children, further work has focused on questions that explore the concepts of materials, energy, forces and light:

(a) Materials: classification and description
    What is the outside of the ice balloon made of? What is the ice balloon itself made of? What does it feel like? What can you see? What does it look like? Why does the balloon split? What are the bubbles inside the balloon? How did they get there? Why is the balloon round? Why has it got a flat part? Why is the surface of the ice balloon misty?

(b) Energy: melting and solidifying
    Why does the ice melt? Does it melt quicker in water? Does it melt differently in water or air? Why does its shape change when it melts in water? Why does it melt quickly when salt is put on it? Why does it refreeze after the salt has been put on? Do the size and shape of the balloon make it melt quicker? Does it melt quicker if we touch it?

(c) Forces
    (i) Floating and sinking
        What happens when we put it in water? Does it float or sink in water? Does it float on the water or under the water? What

happens if you push it under the water? Does it float the same way all the time? Can we change the way it floats? Can we make it sink?

(ii) Friction

Why does the ice balloon slide across the table? Does the ice balloon slide across other surfaces? Why does a paper towel stop it sliding? What happens to the ice balloon as it slides? Does sliding it make it melt quicker?

(iii) Impact

What happens when we drop the ice balloon in the water? What happens when we drop the ice balloon in the playground? Does the height of the drop matter?

(d) Light

What can you see inside the balloon? Can you see through the balloon? How are coloured ice balloons made? What happens if you shine a torch through the balloon? Why can I see through some bits of the balloon and not others?

A group of reception and Year 1 children exploring ice balloons began with their initial observations.

It looks like a big ice cube.
Well, it looks like a balloon that one.
It's got plastic (*referring to the rubber of the balloon*).
It looks like spikes in there.
Looks like frozen glass.

As their observations became more systematic they used large magnifiers and began to see more detail:

There's a hole.
You can still see the spikes.
It's like frozen hair.

I then asked the children what they thought would happen to the ice balloons. A number of ideas emerged here and we were able to explore these further.

They'll break.
Melt if water goes on them.
If you throw them on the concrete floor outside they'll crack.
Me: Why do you think they will crack?
Because the concrete floor is harder than ice.

Relating her ideas to previous experiences, one child commented 'Glass breaks when it goes on the floor.' We then went outside and carefully threw one of the ice balloons across the playground to see what happened, and found that it did crack and shatter on the hard ground.

Later, in the classroom, one child said:

The sun will melt it.
Me: The sun will melt it? Is the sun shining on it here?
No.
Me: Will it stay like this all day?
No, it's going to shrink.
When the rain comes out it will melt.
It melts in water.
Me: Shall we try it and see?

We then got a tank of water and put the ice balloon in. This led to observations and discussions of how the balloon floated in the water.

It floats!
It's heavy! (*pushing it up and down and making it bob*).
The water's warm.
It's shrinking.
It's getting warmer.
It's slippy.
It's getting smaller now.

The children then hypothesized that the balloon in the tank would melt faster than the one on the table and so it was left in the tank while they focused on the other one. Later they noticed its change in shape.

Oo, it's like a bowl.
It's because it floated on the top.
That bit's in the water and that bit's out (pointing).

They took it out of the tank and looked closely at it and then they put it back in the water. It flipped over, so that the previously submerged part, which had melted quickly, was now above the water.

It looks like a big eye.
Look! It's gone sideways.

They seemed aware that it had melted faster under the water than above and related this to their observations about the water temperature. However, they did not seem able to hypothesize why it flipped over, and this could have been a focus for more detailed exploration.

I asked the children what would happen if we put salt on an ice balloon. They responded that it would melt:

Because it's salty.
Because it goes in.

An interesting hypothesis emerged. Lee began by saying 'In the winter, the sea on the ice ... well ice ... winter.' He was then interrupted by another child and later continued:

> Well, I'll tell you about it. The sea that's at the seaside, well they used to be ice. The salt was in it. Then the ice melted into water and now it's salty water. Yeah it's going to make water in here.

This exploration gave the children opportunities to observe, to raise questions which could be explored further, to predict what was going to happen next and to formulate and communicate their hypotheses. The next step would be to help the children to plan investigations arising from these explorations. They could focus on how the ice melts in different situations, on the table, in water, outside, in a refrigerator over a period of time. They could look at the temperature of the ice as it melts, measured either qualitatively or quantitatively or both. They could explore what happens to ice in salty or plain water.

Other explorations could stem from collections. Collections which can be explored include rocks, plants, leaves, toys and musical instruments. Children can explore a collection of seeds such as a coconut, poppy seeds, bean seeds, etc. (as in the garden centre role-play activity in Chapter 1). These could be seeds inside a collection of fruit (as in Handa's Surprise activity described earlier in this chapter) from common examples, such as an apple, an orange and a blackberry, to more unusual ones, such as a kiwi fruit, a pomegranate and a mango. Having been given the collection, they can observe the similarities and differences between the fruiting bodies and/or seeds, notice their characteristics and begin to classify them according to observable features. In doing this, the children can be encouraged to raise questions they can investigate:

- Will all the seeds grow?
- What do the seeds need to grow?
- Do big seeds grow into big plants and small seeds grow into small plants?
- What happens to the fruit/seed if we leave it?
- What part of the seed grows first/next?

Questioning by the teacher can also help formulate simple hypotheses:

- Why do you think the fruits are brightly coloured?
- Why do you think some seeds have got a hard shell?
- Why do you think the root grows first?
- Where do you think the seed gets its food from?

In such a situation, we can begin to find out about the children's ideas and this can enable us to assess their needs and plan activities which will be differentiated according to these needs. We need to remember that this only gives us a snapshot of the children's abilities within one context and as such the assessments we make must be tentative. We are able to indicate their abilities in a particular context, at a particular time, because of evidence we have collected through observation of and interaction with the children. This evidence will enable us to provide future explorations and investigations which will develop or challenge their ideas. In this way, exploration can be used to collect evidence to make informed assessments of the children's development.

A visit to a local shop or supermarket can lead to a vast number of explorations and investigations. During the visit, the children should have the opportunity to observe the different types of product on sale and how they are displayed, packaged and sold. Many shops are happy for children to visit the unseen parts of the shop and witness the different types of work involved. The children should actually buy some goods. This could lead to explorations back in school about the purchases. It may be decided to buy a collection of similar items, such as fresh fruit and vegetables, dairy produce, washing-up liquids, paper towels or biscuits. Back in school, observations and classifications of the produce can occur, according to different criteria such as colour, smell, composition and texture. Further research can later discover the country of origin, the cost per kilogram, etc. With a purchase of fresh fruit and vegetables, close observations can lead to pattern seeking and observational drawings, while explorations can look at whether they float or sink or whether they will grow. The fruit and vegetables can be used for printing or tasting or even in a fruit salad or a stew. Further follow-up work could involve recording favourite tastes in graphical form, designing some packaging for a delicate piece of fruit or a carrier bag for the supermarket, or looking at the recycling and decomposition of packaging. After purchasing different dairy produce, children could look at colour, taste and texture, with further research being carried out to find out how it is processed. Other activities can include using cream to make butter or cottage cheese, with investigations focusing on the time taken to make butter out of different types of cream or whether the processes are reversible or not. A collection of different washing-up liquids could look at observable differences between them (colour, thickness, smell) and proceed to exploring the lathers produced, their ability to make bubbles and the strength of those bubbles and to investigating their success in the removal of stains. This could be set in a familiar context of removing grease stains, food on plates or the staffroom coffee cups! Paper towels can be explored and investigated for absorbency, strength and efficiency.

Biscuits can be explored for taste and flavour, texture, the way they crumble, with the science involved in baking biscuits or the biscuits' strength when dunked as resulting investigations.

Overcoming difficulties in exploratory learning

Our final consideration concerns the difficulties or perceived difficulties of exploratory learning. Early years settings are very complex and have many challenges to meet. These range from,

- the different types of settings (playgroups, nurseries, pre-school, reception, Year 1 and Year 2 classes);
- the need to meet ever increasing and changing demands from the curriculum (Foundation or Key Stage 1);
- different and sometimes seemingly contradictory strategies, such as literacy (DfEE, 1998), numeracy (DfEE, 1999) and the primary strategy (DfES, 2003) advocating excellent teaching and enjoyable learning;
- the different ages of children and developmental stages, sometimes within one class;
- the transitional difficulties the child experiences in moving from one setting and/or one stage of learning and another.

It is hardly surprising that many practitioners faced with so many challenges were confused about what provision for early-years children should look like and began using more prescriptive activities. I believe that an exploratory and less controlled approach has a number of advantages. First, exploration enables us to cover more of the curriculum than prescriptive investigations and in a meaningful way. Exploration allows us to ascertain a child's conceptual needs and to plan specifically for these. With exploration, learning outcomes are more diverse and more closely matched to the children's needs and abilities. In the magnetism work, described earlier in this chapter, the original investigation was designed to focus specifically on which materials were 'magnetic' and which 'non-magnetic'. This rather narrow investigation would only match the needs of a limited number of children. The children who were involved in the investigation had a great many half-formed ideas which the investigation did not clarify, challenge or change. More open-ended exploration led to a wide variety of questions for further investigation, such as what thicknesses of material the magnets would work through, whether the magnet picked up all metals, and whether there are magnets of different strengths. The children began to challenge their existing ideas and formulate new ones.

In another example, children were asked to explore a range of objects connected to the concept of light. These included mirrors and other shiny objects, torches, lenses, old glasses, a kaleidoscope, in fact all the objects that could form part of an interactive display in the classroom on light. Free exploration of these objects led to questions being raised about the concept of light. When looking at her reflection in a spoon Donna asked 'Why is my face upside down this side but the right way here?' When using old glasses to look at writing Jason said 'I can make the writing bigger with these ones,' and Jon noticed that the lenses 'felt different'. Kelly was fascinated by coloured glasses with which she looked at different colours, and this led to exploration using coloured sweet-papers and later to an investigation to see what coloured felt-tip pens she could identify through different coloured wrappers. The initial exploration provided opportunities for differentiation by outcome and led to other activities that could be differentiated by task.

Exploratory activities can also support behaviour management. Whole-class activities which are highly organized and structured may not meet the needs of some children, leading to frustration for those who find the activities difficult and boredom for those who find them conceptually easy. Allowing children the opportunities to explore in ways they chose, allows them to choose the level of difficulty for themselves and is more motivating. So, by being less controlling, we can have greater control of both behaviour and learning. The organization of group and individual exploratory activities can be problematic, but the reality of small-group exploration is easier in practice than whole-class structured teaching, where adult support is stretched thin and more time is spent organizing than interacting. Although some people may feel that exploratory activities need little or no prior planning, this is definitely not the case. Planning needs to be very thorough to allow for every eventuality. Preparation also needs to be excellent to enable the activity to run smoothly. In order to undertake any activity with children, we need to research the concepts and skills involved and consider our feelings and ideas. We then need to make plans so that every avenue will be covered. Even with thorough planning the unexpected avenues of enquiry can still occur, but this creates opportunities for other explorations. This whole process requires some considerable degree of flexibility on the part of the teacher. A student once described to me how the unexpected occurred during an exploration of plasticine and play dough with Key Stage 1 children. He had structured their explorations and in dropping the plasticine and play dough from different heights was hoping to lead on to planning an investigation to look more specifically at the forces involved. Unexpectedly the play dough bounced, and he was concerned that this was not only a deviation from his planning but also had detracted from his intention. It had, however, indicated his inflexibility and, although he soon realized the value of this unexpected exploratory avenue, he was momentarily concerned as to whether he should stick to his original plans or follow a new line of enquiry. On another occasion a student had abandoned all her fine plans for exploratory play activities and was undertaking more directed activities. This was because she was constrained by the enormity of her planning and convinced that she would not cover everything that had to be done.

In this way planning becomes a double-edged sword: we need to plan for every eventuality and to ensure that we have the knowledge to proceed down every avenue of enquiry, but we need to be flexible enough to move away from our plan if the unexpected happens and the learning resulting from that is considered to be beneficial. We know that we do not need to justify why we should abandon planned activities during the one snow shower of the year, so why should we feel the need to justify the desirability of following children's lines of enquiry?

If we do follow children's exploratory ideas, the role of the teacher, during exploration, will be crucial. The teacher's role, which will be discussed further in Chapter 6, should be to encourage, to challenge and to suggest, but not to dominate. Exploratory science activities may require more teacher input than prescriptive activities, but this can be justified by the increased learning involved.

The final difficulty of undertaking exploratory activities is concerned with the confidence of the teacher. Teachers need to have confidence that this approach to teaching and learning is justified by the learning outcomes. Such confidence will allow them to justify it to others, especially parents and governors who may wish to see evidence of the children's work. Teachers also need to have confidence to undertake activities with no apparent structure or organization and no predetermined ending. I use the word 'apparent' carefully here because exploration does not mean a lack of planning, organization or a predetermined ending. Rather, it implies planning and organization towards a number of predetermined endings, all within a recognized learning aim, and the flexibility to modify the planning and organization if that aim can be better met.

Summary

Exploration is important in the early development of scientific skills, knowledge and attitudes. It can be a useful tool:

- in developing the skills of observing, raising questions, classifying, hypothesizing and communicating;

- in developing ideas for further exploration and investigation;
- in matching the conceptual needs and abilities of children and in planning differentiated activities to meet individual needs (see Chapter 6);
- in developing scientific understanding (see Chapter 3);
- in developing attitudes in children (see Chapter 4).

Teachers need to have confidence in exploration as an important part of the learning process of young children and to plan exploratory experiences in the classroom.

3

Knowledge and understanding of the world

Science involves knowing and understanding the world in which we live; it involves understanding scientific phenomena and the ability to use scientific knowledge to make decisions, and to solve problems in a variety of contexts. For example, in order to bake a cake, we need to have some knowledge about materials and how they change when mixed, heated or cooled. In order to make decisions about local transport policies, we need to know about the effect of these policies on the local environment; plants, animals and humans, as well as the effects of pollution on the environment. Young children's knowledge and understanding of the world or scientific knowledge and understandings develop as they explore the world around them. As they experience scientific phenomena, they develop conceptual ideas or mental models of the world which are stored in their long-term memory. They can then access this knowledge when faced with new experiences which will cause them to add to their ideas or modify them or sometimes they may change these ideas.

Figure 3.1 What is knowledge and understanding of the world?

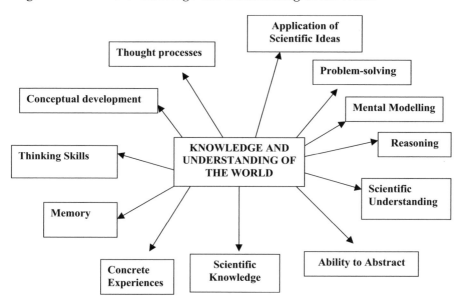

Cognitive theories and science

In Piaget's theory of cognitive development (1929) the constructions of scientific understandings involves the building up of mental structures called schemas (mental representations) and operations (combinations of schemas). All development occurs in the same order; that is the child moves through the stages in order (invariant functioning). However each individual has different experiences and so their cognition will vary (variant functioning). Piaget's observations of his own children's development identified four stages of cognitive development (see Table 3.1), which have generally stood the test of time and further research, although his theories are not without their critics. The idea of stages is sometimes felt to be too absolute and that children's development is more gradual. Further studies have shown that children have understanding of conservation at five or six years of age (Bruner *et al.*, 1956), can think logically at earlier ages, while some adults are never able to achieve logical, abstract thought. I certainly have many experiences of children within the early years who show evidence of abstract thought. For example, while making climbing toys with Year 2 children (see Figure 5.4), I have shown a completed toy to the children and asked them to make a toy for themselves (the man climbs up the string if made correctly and the straws on his arm are angled outwards). Many children quickly make them but they do not work properly and so I ask them to see how their toy differs from mine. They often use large amounts of plasticine, long strings and do not angle the straws correctly, all of which do not make for successful climbers. When they look carefully, they are usually able to see the differences and begin to understand how the toy works. I then ask them to try to work out how the climbing man could climb down the string rather than up it. Many children come to me with ideas without trying these ideas out and have clearly the beginnings of some mental models of how the toy works. They may suggest that you turn the man upside down or add more plasticine and they can try these ideas out to see if they work. A few children will have the correct idea and have not arrived at this by concrete means but by abstract thought.

Despite the ability of children for abstract thought at an earlier age than identified by Piaget, his stages of cognitive development are still useful for understanding children's scientific thinking.

Table 3.1 Piaget's stages of cognitive development and scientific understanding

Stage	Age	Description
Sensori-motor	0–2	Much behaviour is reflexive, for example, babies turn towards sounds and touch. Their first ideas developed about the world are action schemas. They assimilate information through their senses and via experiences. In this way they learn about scientific phenomena by extending and modifying schemas (accommodation), building up mental pictures of the world.
Pre-operational	2–7	Children's thought processes are developing but are not necessarily ordered and logical. They are very egocentric, believe that everything has a consciousness (animism) and all moving objects are alive. They also believe that their opinions are correct (moral realism).
Symbolic	2–4	Children recognize symbols which have meaning (e.g. words, signs, etc.). Language becomes important in mental imagery and understanding about the world.
Intuitive	4–7	The child's perceptions dominate their thinking, which shows a lack of reversibility. Changes in objects mean that there are changes in quantity/

number. They are unable to think about several features of an object at once (conservation) and will be unable to sort using a number of criteria at the same time or handle variables in scientific investigation.

Concrete operational	7–11	Children's thinking gradually becomes more co-ordinated, rational and adult-like. At this stage, egocentric thought declines as does animism. Children can think logically if they can manipulate the object that they are thinking about. Appearance of objects influences thought, so a large object will be thought of as heavy and will make a loud sound. Children are unlikely to change their ideas unless persuasive evidence is present.
Formal operational	11–16	Children begin to rely more on ideas than the need to manipulate objects. Their thinking becomes more abstract. They are able to solve mental problems and to build up mental models of the world. Formal operations involve propositions, hypotheses, logical relationships and contradictions. They are able to see and manipulate variables involved in investigations.

The first of Piaget's stages is the sensori-motor stage. Young children are very egocentric at this time, and are at first relatively unaware of the world around them. They appear to be limited by their simple reflex responses. They can suck and swallow, their heads move towards the warmth of the human body, their arms and legs move around in an uncontrolled manner. Soon, however, they are able to focus their eyes and recognize patterns. They recognize the human face, and this becomes a dominant part of their world. Piaget believes that at this stage children are unable to distinguish between themselves and the rest of the world. This is evidenced by their inability to recognize the existence of an object once it has been removed or hidden. As their awareness develops they are increasingly able to recognize that objects not in sight do exist and can follow an object even when it is not always visible. In this way a young child dropping a toy out of a pram will be aware of the existence and the movement of the toy even when it has fallen away from sight. The child may not remember the fallen toy for long or be aware of the possible consequences of dropping it, but when the toy has fallen the child will often look down for it, recognizing the effects of gravitational force. As their awareness develops, children also become more co-ordinated and their movements less erratic. They learn to pick up objects and experience differences in shape, size and texture. By trial and error they are able to solve simple problems. Early toys encourage them to press buttons, fit objects into slots and generally explore a variety of phenomena. In doing this, children are developing ideas about the world around them. Each new experience allows them to add to their understanding and build up more complex ideas about the world around them.

As children progress from the sensori-motor stage of development they move into the pre-operational stage, which is divided into two sub-stages; symbolic and intuitive. In the symbolic sub-stage language becomes important in mental imagery and understanding about the world. Vygotsky's theories (1962) about language and thought, developed from Piaget's symbolic sub-stage, identify a strong inter-relationship between language and thought, although they are different functions which develop separately. As children begin to speak, they can articulate their ideas and this in turn supports their thinking and consolidates their ideas. At the intuitive sub-stage, language continues to develop and support thinking and mental imagery. The child's perceptions dominate their thinking and they show a lack of reversibility, being unwilling to change their ideas. Changes in objects mean that there are changes in quantity/number, so changing the shape of a ball of plasticine (which sinks) into a boat shape (which floats) changes the weight/mass of the plasticine. Children will also be unable to think about several features of an object at once (conservation) and will be unable to sort using a number of criteria at the same time or handle variables in scientific investigation. This supports the argument that scientific investigation is more appropriate for children at a higher level of conceptual development and that early-years children should be engaged in exploration.

At the concrete operational stage of development, children's thinking gradually becomes more co-ordinated, rational and adult-like. They become less egocentric and more inclined to listen to the ideas of others. This, however, is a slow process and one that involves careful and sensitive interaction. Children are able to think logically if they can manipulate the object that they are thinking about and so thought is very linked to actions. Clearly, at this stage scientific learning needs to be very experiential to enable children to develop, modify or change their ideas. Constructivist theories of the development of scientific understandings (Driver, 1983; Scott, 1987), have developed from Piaget's cognitive theory and advocate the belief that children construct their own meaning from experiences and learning. Making sense of the world is not just about adding to and extending existing ideas, but modifying existing ideas or even radically changing them. Children make sense of the world when they are allowed to construct their own meaning through experience, play, social interaction and by observing phenomena. This is an active and continuous process whereby children construct links with their prior knowledge, generating new ideas, checking and restructuring old ideas or hypotheses, in a very active way. As they develop, they move away from simplistic ideas towards a more sophisticated and scientifically acceptable view of the world, although at this stage children are unlikely to change their ideas unless persuasive evidence is present.

The final stage of Piaget's cognitive theory is the formal operational stage of development. This is the stage during which children are preparing for operations or actions in the mind. These actions are often similar at first to the physical actions carried out in the earlier stages, but now children can carry them out in their minds rather than by physical means. Children begin to group, separate, order and combine in their minds in order to make sense of the world around them. These 'mind actions' can then be carried out in the physical world. At this stage children are beginning to plan for future actions, and this will have obvious use in their scientific development. For example, children will be able to predict that some objects will float in water and others will sink, but with some objects they will still need concrete experiences or to find out by trial and error. Their scientific ideas are subject to change and need reinforcement and considerable support to develop in a scientifically accepted way.

Another set of cognitive theories are also proving to be influential in education and learning. These are the factor theories, initially identified by Spearman (1927) and developed by Thurstone & Thurstone (1941) and Gardener (1983). These recognize that there are a number of different factors or intelligences affecting cognition. Gardener identifies eight different factors:

1. bodily-kinaesthetic or using the body to solve problems and express ideas and feelings;
2. interpersonal or the ability to gauge moods, feelings and needs;
3. intrapersonal or the ability to use knowledge about themselves;
4. linguistic or the ability to use words, oral or written;
5. logical-mathematical or the ability to understand and use numbers and reason well;
6. musical;
7. naturalist intelligence or the ability to organize and classify both the animal and plant kingdoms as well as showing understanding of natural phenomena;
8. spatial or the ability to perceive the visual-spatial world accurately.

Scientific understanding could be argued to depend on the interaction of a number of these factors, even though they may be unrelated. For example, logical-mathematical ability is the core of understanding about the abstract physical world, but spatial ability enables mental models to be developed and linguistic ability or bodily-kinaesthetic abilities are keys to the expression of this understanding. There may also be some factors that are cultural or educationally favoured. For example, Western culture and education favours linguistic and logical-mathematical abilities. Johnston (1996) also identified cognition as multidimensional. Her theory is that there are four interactive learning schemas, which combine together in different ways in individual learners:

- sequential processing or the ability to be ordered, organized and having the desire for clear instructions and time to complete work;
- precise processing or the ability to be precise and detailed and desiring information and enjoying acquiring knowledge;
- technical processing or the ability to be practical, technical or scientific and liking hands-on projects and first-hand experience;
- confluent processing or the ability to be creative or artistic and having confidence in themselves and liking to use imagination and take risks.

She argues that primary teachers are more likely to be sequential and precise and to teach in a way that advantages children who have similar abilities. Children who are more technical and confluent, but find it difficult to be ordered and precise may have very good scientific understandings but may not succeed in formal educational situations. This implies that for many of our children, those with more technical and confluent traits, education is a difficult experience and success is less likely. Practitioners who fail to provide for the technical and confluent learners are likely to fail some children they should be supporting.

Factors affecting children's knowledge and understanding of the world

There are a number of factors that can affect children's early scientific understandings. These include children's prior experiences and understandings, our own understanding of the scientific concepts, their language development, the types of experiences they have and the way we interact with them.

Children's prior experiences

Children in the early years, even at the age of three or four, will have had a variety of experiences which will influence their developing concepts, knowledge, skills and attitudes in science. These experiences will differ in type and context, as will their abilities to make sense of their experiences and the type and quality of the interactions within the experiences. As a result, each child is an individual with individual ideas and needs. We could say that all children have their own unique intellectual fingerprint. Each child is unique, and so we need to know as much about individual children as possible. We need to identify their skills, their attitudes and their scientific ideas. We also need to know about the experiences that have helped their development. This does not mean that we need to teach each child individually, but rather that we should recognize that each child is an individual with specific needs and abilities. Children can be grouped according to their needs and abilities, either to support and encourage development or because they have similar needs. In working with young children we need to recognize that they are not devoid of any scientific, conceptual understanding, skills or feelings about science. We need also to analyse children's ideas and behaviour and tentatively make decisions about the types of experience that will benefit them.

Understanding children's ideas

Explorations can identify for us conceptual areas in need of clarification, modification or development. To do this successfully, we need to have a clear understanding of the relevant concept ourselves and be able to identify the common ideas held by children. There is a plethora of very useful research on children's ideas that we can draw upon. Much of this has been carried out with older children, for example, the research resulting from the Children's Learning in Science (CLIS) project at Leeds University's Centre for Studies in Science and Mathematics Education, and the Primary Science Processes and Concept Exploration (SPACE) project at Liverpool University's Centre for Research in Primary Science and Technology (CRIPSAT) and King's College London's Centre for Educational Studies. However, we can use it as a base for our own practitioner research in the early years. In this way, we are able to begin to identify the way in which young children think and this will enable us to perceive the ideas from a child's perspective and assist them in their explorations and the development of scientific concepts. This perspective will reflect the child's previous experiences and may be very limited in nature. Children have fewer experiences to bring to any situation than adults, and often things adults take for granted can be confusing and create misconceptions. As a result, in all explorations, we need to take care that we look carefully at the children's developing ideas from their perspective. The constructivist teaching sequence advocated by Scott (1987) suggests that practitioners should begin by introducing the concept to the children and then finding out about their existing ideas, before planning activities and experiences to match children's needs, that is to develop, modify or change ideas as appropriate. Learning is not simply a matter of adding to and extending existing concepts. It may necessitate radical reorganization of existing thinking. We should also remember that children may resist new ideas, hold contradictory ideas or even change their ideas depending on the context. In familiar contexts children may develop new or more sophisticated ideas but revert to more simplistic ideas in an unfamiliar context.

In this way learning in science is not passive and children have ownership over their own learning. The first phase of constructivist learning is the orientation phase, where the concept is examined and children's ideas are elicited. Elicitation and subsequent analysis can inform practitioners about children's ideas. Elicitation of ideas and understanding can take the form of analysis of children while they are engaged in science activities and analysing their discourse, actions, pictures and writing. Concept maps can also help us to understand children's ideas. Concept maps (Novak and Gowan, 1984) look similar to 'brainstorming' spiders' webs used to map out ideas for planning. However, they are more organized than these spiders' webs, in that they indicate perceived relationships between concepts. Children can use an already prepared list of words related to a concept or brainstorm their own. These words are then linked using appropriate words.

Andrew's first attempt at a concept map (Figure 3.2) is very simple but shows his thinking on the theme of ice. It is important to find time to discuss with children the ideas they have expressed in their maps and this will help to confirm initial analysis. Further analysis of Andrew's map indicated that he saw the process of melting and solidifying as a one-way process, and it was important to clarify this before planning and further development could continue. The discussion with Andrew about his concept map was essential to elicit his ideas. The map alone can only give an indication of his thinking.

The next phase in constructivist learning involves the restructuring of ideas. This may involve the children in situations where their ideas are challenged and refuted, and this may cause some frustration. It is important that each child experiences some success and that any feelings of frustration are harnessed to motivate and not de-motivate. It is also important that children have opportunities to reflect on their old ideas and emerging new ideas. New or modified ideas are fragile and need

Figure 3.2   Andrew's concept map

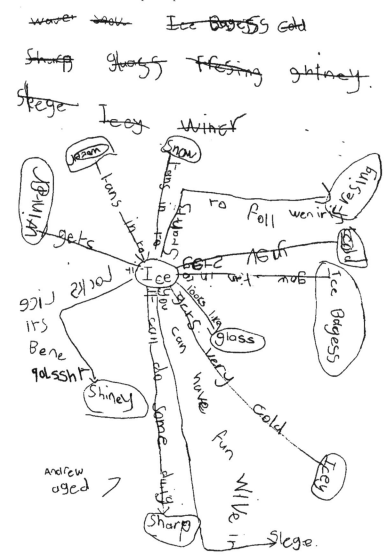

nurturing. The children need time to consider them and opportunities to apply them in other situations. This will not only help to clarify ideas but to develop them further. As children's ideas are developed and reviewed they will be able to use them in a variety of situations both familiar and unfamiliar. They should also be able to link complex and abstract phenomena together. For older children, revisiting their original concept maps at this stage can be useful to consolidate new ideas developed through teaching.

While working with children in the early years, I have discovered some of these alternative ideas, which illustrate the way they think and how these ideas are affected by their experiences. Children will have been exposed to the concept of 'light' from the moment of birth (unless they have visual problems). We know that young babies do not have the same vision as adults and that there are individual differences in colour vision, but all visually-sound children will have experienced light from a variety of sources, shadows, mirrors and optical illusions. Some children will have spectacles and so experience lenses and many will have used magnifiers in explorations or seen distorted images through glass of different shape. When exploring light with Foundation Stage children, I set up activities exploring,

- shadows, using a shadow puppet theatre;
- reflection, using bubbles, kaleidoscopes and mirrors;
- illusions, using lenses, coloured acetates and different glasses.

During the explorations and in discussions with children, I identified a number of interesting ideas. One child talked about her white melamine wardrobe as source of light, as she would lie in bed and see the light from outside reflected off it. Most children believed that shadows would be 'best' (darkest) if made out of black paper and dismissed shadows made by transparent acetate as 'not shadows'. They recognized the transparent and reflective quality of a bubble, saying that it was 'see-through' but also that they could see themselves in the bubble, both upside down and the 'right-way up'. However, the children believed that square blowers would make square bubbles or that bubbles could only be made from round bubble-blowers! When looking through lenses and in concave mirrors and seeing an inverted image, they would consistently turn the lens around to try to get the image the 'right way up'. I have also seen this with children of all ages when looking at a camera obscura – a shoe box with a greaseproof paper sheet over the open end (or inserted into the lid) and a magnifying lens over a hole in the bottom. You need to make sure that the focal distance of the lens is the same as the width of the shoe box and then images from around the room or through a window can be seen on the greaseproof sheet. This image is upside down and children will turn the box around in order to get a 'right-way up' image.

Sometimes children not only develop alternative ideas or misconceptions, they also appear to take a backward step in their understandings. We expect that their developing ideas will become more sophisticated and scientific as they develop, but instead of being linear, the development of some ideas appears to develop as a U-shaped curve

Picture 3.1 *Children exploring light through shadow puppets and a camera obscura*

(Strauss, 1981). In science, this trend has been seen in children of all ages and results from early intuitive ideas being developed as a result of experience and interaction with scientific phenomena into, what appears to be, less scientifically accurate ideas. If we ask children to identify animals from a range of pictures or real animals, including fish, minibeasts (spiders, ants, worms), mammals (rabbit, whale, cat, dog), we get surprisingly odd results, with younger children apparently giving more correct responses than older children. Young children's responses are based on their limited experience and intuitive ideas. Animals have certain physical characteristics, such as movement, mouth, eyes, etc. As they get older their ideas become more sophisticated and they develop personal theories about the world, based on further experience and interaction. They begin to understand that living things can be grouped according to certain features and characteristics, such as fish, minibeasts and mammals or even that ants are insects, spiders are arachnids, whales are mammals but live in the sea like fish. As a result of the development of these more sophisticated ideas about the living world, children sometimes become confused and, knowing that a whale is a mammal or an ant is an insect, they will not identify them as animals and so apparently make a backward step cognitively. It is only as their ideas become even more sophisticated and their understanding of the concept is more secure, that they can answer correctly from an informed base.

Another example of children's personal and scientifically incorrect theories about the world, is the idea that heavy things will fall more quickly than light things. This scientifically incorrect idea is based on their observations of the world around them; they see 'light' feathers, leaves, paper falling slower than 'heavier' conkers, twigs, toys. We can give them a range of objects of similar shapes and sizes and different masses to drop to show that they fall at the same rate or even take a flat and screwed up piece of paper and drop them at the same time. However, when the children have developed a personal theory, they are often very reluctant to change their idea and will ignore or try and explain results which do not fit their theories. Early-years children for example, will tell you that when you screw up a piece of paper you make it heavier!

Language development

Another factor affecting children's understandings in science is their language development. Scientific vocabulary has often different meanings in everyday life and this can lead to difficulties in understanding scientific concepts. The word 'weight' (a force exerted on something due to gravity) is used when we mean mass (an amount of material). The word 'energy' is used to imply a fuel, which can be used up. The word 'material' (a substance in the material world) is commonly used to mean fabric, although to a technologist it would mean different types of materials (textile, metal, wood, etc.). On one occasion, at the end of a five-week study on 'light' a student teacher asked a class to name some light sources. A child responded with 'low fat mayonnaise'! There are many other words and phrases for which children have alternative scientific conceptual meanings, such as 'melting' in place of 'dissolving', 'hole in the ozone layer', meaning a physical hole in the sky and 'the greenhouse effect', a phrase which appears more confusing than helpful to a young child.

Language development can also affect children's communication of their understandings. In the early years children need to be able to communicate their emergent ideas and the only way they can effectively do this is orally (QCA, 2000). Oral articulation also helps children to make sense of their developing ideas. They should be given opportunities to describe scientific phenomena in their own words and this will support their further scientific development, especially as they are introduced to new words and more scientific meanings as appropriate. If children find it difficult to articulate their scientific understandings, because of physical disabilities, or shyness or any other cause, we need to be patient and to give them time and support to express the ideas they hold. I was once working with Year 1 children in Brazil in sorting fabrics according to whether they were suitable for hot or cold weather. The children had to sort a suitcase of clothes for teddy and dress him according to whether he was going to Brazil or England and to use fabric squares to dress a teddy outline. One boy dressed his teddy outline for Brazil with sun-glasses and light-weight clothes, including aluminium foil trousers. His teacher thought that he had recognized the reflective qualities of the foil, but discussion with him identified that teddy was dressed for a carnival party!

Towards the end of the early years, children will begin to write down their scientific ideas or results of explorations and investigations and they are sometimes hindered by their limited use of language. As they may not have the words in their vocabulary or be able to spell words they would like to use, they may use words that are not accurate reflections of their

Picture 3.2 *Dressing teddy pictures*

scientific understanding. Also, the process of writing may have more to do with English than science and do little to support the achievement of scientific learning objectives. In the observation of Year 2 children described in Chapter 2, they were filling in worksheets about the magnetic properties of materials, which did not allow for precision and accuracy and led children to believe that all metals were magnetic.

Explorations of materials have identified language problems in young children. I often begin such explorations with a mixed bag of household shopping. This can lead to children's explorations involving classification according to material properties (hard, soft, squidgy, rough, smooth, liquid, solid, gas), origin (naturally occurring, man-made, processed, plant, animal, country) or use (washing, eating, making). When exploring materials, confusions can arise because some words have different meanings in a scientific context than in everyday use. For example, what does the word 'material' mean to a child? Does it mean matter, textiles, fabric? I once asked a child who had been asked to write a sentence using the word 'liquid' what she thought the word meant. She was quite confident in her answer that it was 'something that was used for washing up or was used in washing machines'; her understanding being specific rather than seeing liquid in its generic sense. In the same way, what does a child think a gas is? A fuel for fires and cookers? Does a child consider both a piece of wood and a ball of plasticine to be solid? They do not look the same; one is malleable and the other is not; one is hard and the other is not, but both are considered solid in the scientific sense.

Another cause of confusion may occur when exploring naturally occurring or man-made materials as this is an abstract idea which many children will not have experienced and will have no clear definition of the terms. I well remember my daughter, at about five years of age, telling me in amazement that her grandmother made chips from potatoes! In our bag of shopping we need to realize that most naturally occurring products are processed by man and look decidedly dissimilar to their natural state. For example, a can and a sheet of foil made of aluminium look dissimilar and neither looks like a lump of bauxite; cardboard does not look like a tree; cheese does not look like milk; and plastic does not look like oil. If the aim in our explorations is to consider whether the material is naturally occurring, man-made or processed, we need to have a range of artefacts for comparison which include material in its natural state and, where possible, materials within the children's experience – for example, sheep's wool, rocks, tree branches or twigs – otherwise we need to change our criteria for classification to include naturally occurring materials which have been processed by man. This obviously changes the nature of exploration with a bag of shopping, but we need to be prepared for the possible ideas emerging from such an exploration.

From such a starting point, other materials in their natural state or processed in a different way can be introduced. Follow-up work with a bag of shopping often involves simple baking investigations to see if the materials change during the baking process and to consider whether these changes are reversible or not. Materials in the bag of shopping that are considered to exhibit a reversible change of state when heated or cooled (for example, chocolate and butter) can be compared with others that are considered to be irreversible (for example, eggs and fruit). To a child some of these reversible changes are confusing and again they have little understanding of the term 'reversible'. In addition, their observations will tell them that the material has changed significantly. After all, a bar of chocolate or a pat of butter melted and allowed to cool does not look the same after these changes even if in scientific terms it is a reversible change.

Practitioner interaction

It is important to remember that children's conceptual scientific understanding, whether influenced by different factors or developed in stages, does not occur regardless of experiences and interaction. Children's knowledge and understanding of the world will occur only if experiential opportunities are made available to them, and informed adults interact with them in an appropriate manner (see Chapter 5). The importance of sensitive interaction is recognized by Vygotsky (1962), who identified how expert adults can interact with learners (zone of proximal development) in ways suited to age, culture and social needs. The zone of proximal development is described by Harlen (2000a: 162–3) as 'an area just beyond current understanding (where a person is in conscious control of ideas and knows he or she is using them) where more advanced ideas can be used with help'. Skilled adult interaction or scaffolding can help the learner move beyond their initial ideas and develop their conceptual understanding. It is also a principle underpinning the Foundation Stage Curriculum (QCA, 2000: 12) which asserts that 'effective learning and development for young children requires high-quality care and education by practitioners'. In this way, a wide range of experiential and interactive opportunities should be made available from an early age to encourage development. As children are individuals, with individual experiences, ideas, abilities and needs, they also need different types of interaction. It is therefore important that practitioners are flexible in their interactions, being aware when and how it is best to be involved in the child's explorations and when it is better to give children space and time to explore for themselves. In the garden centre play, described in

Chapter 1, one child did not respond to adult interaction and preferred to explore the seed collection, quietly and individually, while another sought out adult interaction, asking questions and involving adults and other children in his play.

In some explorations, children may need specific interactions to support or stretch their learning, because of specific abilities or because prior experiences or cultural influences have led them to specific understandings. Cultural influences on understandings can be very diverse, involving language, independence and experiences. Clearly, if children are interacting in a second language, this will affect both the quality of the interactions with adults and peers and the way they express their scientific ideas. Children in Brazil who were dressing teddy for different weathers, did not have the words for warm weather clothing, such as scarf and gloves, and Asian children have needed to use their own language to describe materials, when they have not had English alternatives. Finnish children have shown greater independence when exploring a collection of fruit, while Bosnian children have expected more direction and to be led by the practitioner. Brazilian children expect a great deal of emotional motivation and tactile interaction and in England we are expected to interact in a detached way to ensure child security. Children who experience cultural conflict for any reason are likely to have difficulties in some explorations and this needs to be taken into consideration by practitioners. Many student teachers with whom I work appear to have a very didactic and inflexible approach to teaching, which places the teacher at the centre of the interaction and does not allow for child-centred exploration with the adult as an involved facilitator. Such an approach will not provide the necessary experiences or interaction for conceptual development.

Sometimes our interactions can have an adverse affect on the developing ideas and lead children to inaccurate ideas about the world. Research (Watt and Russell, 1990) has shown that six-year-old children believe that big objects make loud sounds and small objects quiet sounds. I have seen some very creative movement lessons, where children are asked to make big movements to loud sounds and small movements to quiet sounds, which I believe, has influenced this alternative idea. Teaching about growing plants can also lead children to alternative conceptions of the world, which can have profound effects later in their scientific development. It is a common belief among children of all ages, and indeed many adults, that plants grow by taking in food from the soil, through their roots. Some early interactions, especially where they are more teacher-led can make it very difficult later in the children's lives when they are expected to rethink their ideas and understand the difficult and abstract concept of photosynthesis (green plants turning the carbon from the air into carbon in their cells, using the energy from the sun). The problem with some early interactions is that we often ask young children to explore the factors that affect growth, a difficult concept, as young children are not able to handle more than two variables at a time. When we do this we consider light, soil and water, but often fail to identify air as a factor, because it is difficult to show how air is important for growth. We also often fail to support children in their understanding as to why these factors are important and so children think light or the sun is for warmth rather than energy. This alternative idea is supported by the fact that seeds grow in the dark (because they have energy stored inside their cells). Children may also think soil is needed for food rather than for support and some nutrients. If we mention air as a factor for growth the children think it is needed to 'breathe', rather than for respiration (not breathing) as well as for growth. Educational activities designed to develop understanding of plant growth often include activities that are not good science or education and that perpetuate alternative conceptions. For example, we germinate seeds in different conditions to show that plants need light to grow, even though seeds do not need light to germinate as they have all the energy they need for germination stored in them. We also investigate the effects of soil, air and water on plant growth and make generalized conclusions about plant growth from these specific instances, when many plants have different needs and importantly the main factor needed for growth, air, is not mentioned.

As a result of interactions and formal teaching, young children will often change or modify their intuitive ideas. However, these synthetic ideas, modified as a result of experiences, interactions and teaching may still not be scientifically accurate. One example of this concerns children's ideas about day and night. Young children think that the sun goes away during the night and the moon goes away during the day. Interactions, which involve the children in observing the moon during the day, shadows at different times of the day, fiction books and even holidays to different countries can challenge the children's intuitive ideas and they may recognize the earth as moving but still see the sun and moon as interchangeable. Another example is that children's intuitive ideas that heavy things sink and light things float can be modified through interactions so that they believe they can change the mass of an object by changing its shape or make a ball of plasticine lighter by moulding it into a boat shape.

The development of thinking skills

Encouraging children to develop their own ideas on scientific phenomena and supporting them in developing mental models can help not only with specific scientific understandings, but with generic thinking skills, which can support children throughout their lives. Mental modelling involves children in developing their own ways of expressing a phenomenon, rather than being given an analogy to support understanding (Bliss *et al.*, 1992). If children are given an analogy they may often develop alternative conceptions, which are hard to challenge. For example, one child I worked with thought that magnets were made up of little strings of 'sausage-like' metal, because they had been given this analogy to explain magnetism. They were also convinced that if they broke a magnet the 'sausages' would fall out and that magnet would lose its magnetism. Apart from being too advanced a concept for a young child, this analogy did not advance their scientific thinking. It is better to introduce a wide range of activities to encourage the children to think for themselves. This can be done by working with the children to solve problems and develop understanding of the cause and effect of scientific phenomena. Early-years thinking skills can be developed by:

- challenging children ideas, by getting them to test out their hypotheses;
- setting problems for them to solve;
- discuss their ideas and compare with the ideas of others;
- encourage them to make causal links.

For example, children who think that older children are taller than younger ones, thick material will keep things warm but not cold or heavy things sink or fall to the ground more quickly can be encouraged to test out their ideas. They will not come to a complete scientific understanding of the underlying concepts but that is unimportant. What is important is that they have the opportunity to reconsider their ideas as a result of evidence. Simple problems can be solved while the children are playing. An optician's can give the children opportunities to explore lenses and colours, provide a range of glasses (sun-glasses, magnifying glasses, glasses with coloured lenses) and allow the children to explore how things look different through them. This will give the children opportunities to develop generalized ideas about the way we see.

   Children need to be aware that they have ideas and that these ideas are valid. Practitioners need to provide opportunities for children to discuss their ideas and make them aware of their own ideas (Brown *et al.*, 1997) and those of others. Discussion of ideas is recognized as important for thinking in science in the early years (Keogh and Naylor, 2000) and in older children (Jones, 2000). Indeed, Costello (2000: 87) identifies argument as *'one of the central objectives of* education'. Through their explorations, problem-solving and discussions the children can be encouraged to try to explain their ideas, think hypothetically (de Bóo,

1999) and make causal links between phenomena and their hypothetical ideas. They can also identify their metacognitive processes, that is, how they solved problems or the thinking behind their interpretations and hypotheses (Fisher, 2003).

There are some gender differences in thinking skills, which can be seen in the early years (see Table 4.1). Girls are likely to have more developed language skills and therefore will be able to articulate their emerging ideas more fully. Boys tend to have better spatial abilities and so are more able to produce their own mental models.

Some exploratory ideas to develop scientific thinking

A collection of electrical items used in a nursery with three- and four-year-old children created enthusiasm and opportunities to explore existing ideas. The resources included wires with simple socket and plug connections, 1.5 volt bulbs, 1.5 volt batteries, some switches, buzzers and a motor. All the children knew what was needed to make a bulb light up:

Electric.
Put wires in it.
You need batteries.
You have to plug it in here.

Unlike other explorations the children wanted considerable direction and to be told 'how to do it', and lighting the bulb became rather competitive. After some exploring Richard managed to make a circuit and exclaimed 'I'm the winner'. As other children lit their bulbs there were cries of 'Mine's brighter' and 'Mine's better'. There was also little interest in sharing resources with other children. While this provided opportunities to develop skills in working with others, care needed to be taken to ensure that every child had a fair chance to explore. When the circuit did not work the children tended to say 'The battery is wrong' or 'It's broken', not being curious enough to try to find out how it worked or change the battery and not seeing failure as a normal part of everyday life and an important stimulus to success and understanding. On another occasion, student teachers found that a buzzer would not work, not realizing that buzzers are a 'one-way system' and need to be wired up correctly (with the red wire to the positive terminal and the black to the negative terminal). I am unsure as to why electrical explorations illustrate this lack of curiosity and tentative ideas, but I think that some of the problems occur because,

- of the complex and abstract nature of the concept. We can see the effects of electricity but not the electricity itself.
- different voltage bulbs will vary the brightness in the circuit leading to confusion about the electricity. Even 1.5 volt bulbs may vary in actual voltage, leading to ideas about electricity in the circuit being used up.
- components which do not work lead children to assume they are broken and they do not try to find out why they do not work.
- batteries that run out make children think that we can run out of energy.
- battery and bulb holders do not allow children to see how the electricity moves around a circuit. Especially problematic are double battery holders, where the electricity appears to go in and out of the battery the same way.

Later in her explorations of electrical components, Lucy found that she could make her light go on and off and this led to exploration of switches. 'That's a switch' said Richard, and Zoe picked up a switch and said, 'Like this'. Zoe then put a switch into her circuit. 'Ooo look!' she said when it worked, and then spent a long time turning the bulb on and off. The children were not curious at this stage about the buzzer and motor and did not explore these at all, being satisfied with the bulbs. Richard eventually asked what they were for. I suggested that he put one in his circuit and see. He put the buzzer in with the bulb and found that they did not work. 'I need more electric' he said, and added another battery. With a bit of assistance he made a circuit and was delighted with his buzzer. The noise became very wearying after a while, but he was developing some good ideas about circuits. Luke used the motor and added a foil propeller to make a fan. He spent the next half-hour fanning people in the nursery to 'keep them cool' even though this was late October.

I once put family photographs and photograph albums in the home area of a reception class and put a family tree outline on the wall. The pictures, which included grandparents, parents, aunts, uncles and siblings, were used during play to discuss family members and compare the people in the pictures to the children's families. Similarities and differences between the family members (age, gender, relationships) were discussed and this led to discussion about their families. Through the interaction children were able to see that families were different sizes, with different ages of members. Darshan explained that he lived with his extended family containing elderly grandparents and young nieces and nephews. Kimberley lived in a single parent nuclear family, although her grandparents lived nearby. Josh lived with his parents and baby sister, but all his other relatives lived a long way away. Frankie lived with her mother and stepfather and had step-brothers and sisters who came to stay at weekends. The children were then encouraged to explore the family photographs and put them into the photo album and add photographs to a family tree on the wall of the home area. They noticed how some family members had similar hair colours or looked like each other in different ways and decided relationships between them on this basis. While the children sorted the photographs and added them to the album, they identified to me or other children the reasons for putting the photograph on any particular page of the album or position on the family tree. Josh said that one photograph needed to go first as it was older than the rest. When asked to explain his reasoning, he said that the people in the photograph were younger and so it was an older picture. He said that he had photographs of his 'nana' who looked like his 'mummy' now. Many of the children then brought in baby photographs of themselves and these were displayed on the wall of the home area and the children could identify how they had grown and how changed since they were a baby. Through this play and interaction, the children were able to extend their knowledge about the human life cycle and about similarities and differences between and within families.

On a separate occasion, I explored the insulating qualities of different gloves with Year 2 children. Our collection of gloves included leather, wool, rubber, cotton and latex gloves and the children predicted which one would keep them warmest. Sarbjit predicted that the leather glove would be the warmest, but Paula and Joe thought it would be the woolly one and most children agreed with this. Peta pointed out that her mum used rubber gloves when washing up in hot water and so she thought the rubber glove would make the hand cold. We then tried out our ideas by putting a latex glove filled with warm water into each glove and waited for 30 minutes and then felt them. The children decided that the woolly glove was the best, although the leather one was probably about the same temperature. They were almost certainly influenced by their earlier prediction and I suspect that it would have been very difficult to make them consider alternative ideas. I then asked them which glove they thought would be the best to keep the hands cool and they all thought that the cotton one would be the best and the woolly one would be the worst. I suggested that we put an ice hand into each glove and leave it and see which one melted first. The children all thought that the ice hand in the woolly glove would melt first. They were very surprised to find that the woolly glove kept the ice hand cold and although some explanations for this were offered, such as we did not do it properly, none was based on the evidence.

Children find the reversibility of insulating materials difficult to understand, thinking that if a material is a good insulator, then it will keep warm things warm and warm up cold things. Even when faced with the evidence to the contrary, they will find this a hard concept to understand. However, it will be an experience that they will store away in their long-term memory and when faced with the concept of insulation on another occasion, they will be able to recall these ideas and develop their understanding further.

Supporting the development of children's knowledge and understanding of the world

Children make sense of the world around them through observation and exploration. We can support their understandings of the world by providing opportunities for them to explore their world and construct their understandings from their experiences. The learning environment should be one that encourages cognitive development; 'encompassing milieux, in which the messages of learning and work are manifest and inviting' (Gardner, 1991: 204). These experiences need to be diverse and exploratory for effective development of conceptual understanding. Most importantly children need to be engaged in exploratory play activities as it is through play that children are more likely to develop their ideas. The importance of play for cognitive development is well recognized (Anning, 1991; Moyles, 1994; Bennett *et al.*, 1997; QCA, 2000). Direct teaching is unlikely to support the development of ideas or modification of alternative ideas. This will especially be the situation if the children hold firmly to their ideas and resist changing them. If practical experience is not persuasive, then direct teaching will have little chance. These ideas are discussed further in Chapter 6.

Practitioners also need to ensure that experiences are motivating, as it is motivation that will support children in future learning. Motivating experiences leads to motivated children who want to learn and will take their explorations further, thus developing their ideas. The importance of motivation and the impact it has on cognition has long been realized (Isaacs, 1930). The child's world is full of exciting and interesting scientific phenomena, which we as adults take for granted. It is not difficult to provide a range of interesting and exciting experiences (see Chapter 5 for further discussion and examples). Motivating experiences will help children to develop positive attitudes, such as tolerance of others' ideas, respect for evidence and flexibility and creativity of thought, which will support further development of scientific ideas.

Sometimes children need challenging experiences to encourage them to think more deeply, reconsider and modify ideas. These challenges can be set as small problems to solve, while the children are playing. For example, as described early in this chapter, we can challenge the children to make something that floats (such as aluminium foil or a citrus fruit) sink, or to make something that sinks (such as a ball of plasticine or a marble) float. Scrunching up the foil will increase its density, as will removing the peel and pith of the citrus fruit. It is quite challenging to remove the peel, thus making it smaller but more dense and seeing that it sinks. As well as challenging children, we can question them during their experiences and this will encourage them to think and develop simple hypotheses. When working in a vertically grouped Key Stage 1 class, I asked children why toy cars rolled down a slope. Katharine (aged five) responded that the cars 'just go down', while Gareth (aged six) said that it was because 'the wheels are round' and Craig (aged seven) said that 'the car is on a slope and it just topples down'. Our questioning can also encourage children to question their own ideas and observations. So the children could be encouraged to question what affects the car going down the ramp, such as the slope, the size of the car, the size of the wheels, etc. On another occasion, when a child observed that he could see himself, 'the right way up and the wrong way up' in a bubble, I encouraged him to find other things that did this (shiny spoons, concave/convex mirrors, glass baubles), to look for similarities between these objects and to draw conclusions about why this phenomenon occurred.

Practitioners can also support children's cognitive development by allowing them to develop their ideas about the world around them at their own rate and not an artificially imposed one. This may mean adapting cognitive learning objectives to match individual learning needs or removing artificial obstacles in the way of the developing child or by allowing children to progress at their own rate. For many gifted children this means removing the brakes (Evans, 2002) to allow them to develop in accordance with their ability rather than their age and the notion of cognitive stage. There are arguments against some types of cognitive acceleration, mainly because the rest of the child's development is unlikely to progress at the same rate and this may cause social and emotional problems later in life. Cognitive acceleration is also thought to be supported by Brain Gym (Dennison and Dennison, 1994), which advocates drinking plenty of water and undertaking three minutes of exercise to support left/right brain co-ordination and cognitive development.

While the link between drinking water and brain development is well known and Brain Gym has proved very popular in some classrooms, there are some practitioners who have not found it useful in supporting children's thinking. It may be that any activity that focuses children's energy and encourages them to think will support cognition, so that it is the reflective practice of the adult that is as significant as the Brain Gym activities on the cognitive development of the child.

Developing the whole child

Another argument is that the development of ideas is only part of the development of the whole child. Children need to develop skills, attitudes and conceptual understandings and while this is recognized in the Foundation Stage of Learning (QCA, 2000), it appears less obvious when looking at the National Curriculum (DfEE, 1999) and the QCA Schemes of Work (QCA, 2000a). Additionally, development in one key area or subject area should not be compartmentalized. Children will develop ideas, skills and attitudes in many different areas while engaging in thematic exploratory play. On the theme of holidays, practitioners can set up a travel agency and passport office in the classroom, with travel magazines, holiday brochures, videos of holiday destinations (obtained from the television or given by travel agencies) and a map of the world or globe. Children can choose holiday destinations and find the country on a world map or globe. They can then make their own passports by filling in details on a prepared passport form. This can be very simple for Foundation Stage children (see Figure 3.3) or more complicated by adding additional personal information, such as age, height, weight, address, favourite colour, friend, etc. (see Johnston and Herridge, 2004). The children can draw themselves on the passport or add photographs or insert photographs on to an electronic copy of the passport from a digital camera. This is fairly easy to do. Set up the computer and printer in the passport office and attach a digital camera via the USB port. Open the passport on a word document and then children can take each others photographs using the camera, insert them on to their passport and print it out. The children can then add the other personal details. You can add your school logo and name at the top of the passport. School stamps or other stamps can be used to stamp the passports in the passport office.

Children can also pack a suitcase for their holiday destination, choosing clothes appropriate for the weather in their chosen destination. I usually choose a selection of T-shirts, jumpers, socks, shoes, glasses, hats, scarves and a choice of bags to pack them in. The activity can be extended to include the travelling class teddy who sends postcards back from his holidays. I have travelled with Columbus Bear to Finland and sent back a 15-minute video of Columbus by the freezing sea. He inspired a Finnish teacher to send Christopher Bear to England. I have also taken teddy bears from other schools to Bosnia and Macedonia, encouraging children in schools in each country to learn about each other. Indeed, some schools now have very well-travelled bears, who send postcards from their destinations and the children can track their progress. The activity can be further developed by setting up a seaside in the classroom. This can be done by choosing a corner where sand and seaside objects (shells,

Figure 3.3   Passport for Foundation Stage

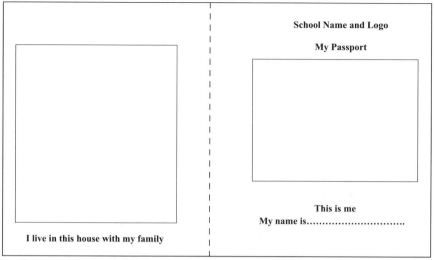

buckets, spades, fishing floats, nets, sponges, flags, windmills, etc) can be set out for the children to play with, sort and experience. The children love to take off their shoes and socks and play in the sand, feeling the texture and even making sand angel pictures on the floor! The water trough and a sand trough (for deeper sand play) can be set nearby and the children can explore wet and dry sand, making castles and explore floating and sinking.

Through this thematic play the children can be developing in the following key areas/subject areas:

Communication, language and literacy/English
Reading holiday brochures
Communicating with others in role-play
Filling in passports (written communication)
Listening to videos
Writing postcards

Knowledge and understanding of the world/science, ICT, geography
Packing the suitcase with clothes for particular weather conditions (sorting materials)
Exploring objects which float or sink (forces and materials)
Exploring wet and dry sand (materials)

ICT
ICT picture for passport using digital camera
Operating computer and video

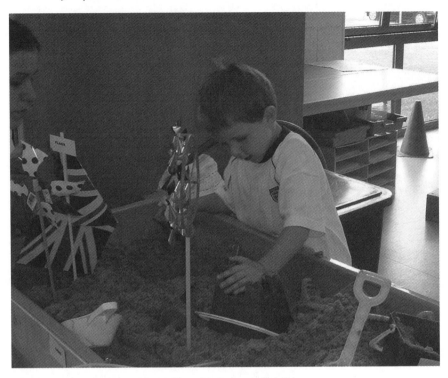

Picture 3.3   *Children playing on the theme of holidays*

Geography
Identifying places in the world
Identifying weather conditions in different places

Personal, social and emotional development
Social interaction

Developing 'difficult' concepts through thematic work

Thematic work is discussed more fully in Chapter 5. Here we look at how themes can be a good way to develop knowledge and understanding of 'difficult' concepts, those ideas that are abstract, inaccessible and difficult to develop as they are often counter-intuitive. Themes can be a good way to focus on these 'difficult' concepts in science. The seaside can be a good opportunity to focus on knowledge and understanding of forces. Children can explore the forces in floating and sinking, observe a Lego man diver (see Figure 5.3), make a diver who climbs up to his boat (see Figure 5.4), explore magnetic forces by playing a magnetic fishing game and make a seaside balancing flag. While making these flags with Year 1 children, I showed children one I had made and they attempted to make their own. The flags are made by putting plasticine into a half table-tennis ball (cut in half using a junior hacksaw before the activity). A flag sellotaped on to a piece of straw is then put into the plasticine so the flag is balanced and will always remain vertical, however pushed or knocked. In order to balance and remain vertical, the flag needs to have a low centre of gravity. If the straw is too long or the flag too big it will be difficult to balance. Most of the children quickly made one, but found it difficult to balance because they used a whole straw, rather than a piece of straw. I directed them to look closely at the one I had made and they began to try out different sized straws, with successful results. They were able to describe in their own words what makes the flag balance:

It needs to be short.
It has to have a little straw.
You need a lot of plasticine to make it stand up.

Picture 3.4   *Children making a balancing flag*

On another occasion I set up a bakery in the Foundation Stage classroom and the children could make and play with dough, focusing on the way the materials change when mixed together or heated (Sc3). The children were encouraged to describe the dough ingredients in their own words, predict what would happen to the materials when mixed or heated and to try to explain what has happened as we make the dough (again in their own words, although new scientific vocabulary can be introduced as appropriate). This will develop important language and communication skills as well as scientific skills and knowledge. The theme can be further developed through a visit to a local bakery or supermarket, which can focus on the technology involved in baking, as some supermarkets allow children to see behind the scenes. Some will also allow children to make bread or pizzas and this can also aid development of material change. The story of *Mr Bembleman's Bakery* (Green, 1978) can support this understanding and provide another link with language and literacy. In the story, the use of non-standard measurements in baking is explored and this can be a link with mathematics.

With Year 2 children I have developed the same ideas through a potions lesson, after Harry Potter (Rowling, 1997), by wearing an academic gown and in role as Snape's supply teacher. I begin as a severe teacher, telling them the dangers of messing around with potions and then encourage the children to predict what will happen if they mix small amounts of substances with water in clear plastic beakers. After predicting, the children try out their ideas and we discuss what has happened and whether this is different to their predictions. I use six mystery solids (salt, sugar, cornflour, talcum powder, bicarbonate of soda and plaster of Paris) and six mystery liquids (white vinegar, detergent, lemonade, cooking oil, lemon juice and colour change bubble bath) in plastic tubs and identified only by labels with symbols, colours, numbers or letters. When mixed with water, the substances will dissolve (salt and sugar), clump (talcum powder), cloud the water (cornflour, bicarbonate of soda, lemon juice), float (oil), sink (plaster of Paris), froth (detergent, bubble bath) or change colour (bubble bath).

Through the theme the scientifically 'difficult' ideas behind changing materials can be explored. At this age children do not need to know about dissolving, melting, reversible changes, or even have well formed definitions of solids and liquids, but they can begin to explore these ideas and this will support them in their later cognitive development.

Another theme which links knowledge and understanding in a number of different areas is music. Through exploration of musical instruments, children can develop understanding of how different sounds are made (see Johnston and Herridge, 2004). I use a range of instruments which make sounds by shaking (for example, maracas, rain-makers, bells),

Picture 3.5 *Exploring materials in the bakery*

banging (for example, tambourines, xylophone), blowing (for example, recorders, panpipes) and plucking (play harps, violins, piano). I introduce the instruments to the children while sitting on the carpet in a circle and we explore how they make sounds, with each child telling a partner how their instrument makes a sound. Follow-up activities include:

- exploring the instruments and sorting them according to how they make the sound or what kind of sound they make (loud, quiet, high, low, rattle, squeak, boom, bang, whistle, etc.);
- making an instrument which makes a sound by banging, shaking, plucking or blowing. Older or more able children can make an instrument which can make a range of notes. These instruments can be decorated by the children to produce a good finished product;
- exploring how they can make their instrument (or a class instrument) make a different sound (higher, lower, quieter, louder).

A group of children can create a piece of music, using either the class instruments or their own. This can be performed to others in the class and/ or recorded on a tape recorder. Questioning the children can help to ascertain whether they can make a loud, quiet, high or low sound and describe what they did.

In this way the children would be developing learning in science, technology and music (Key Stage 1) or in the key areas of knowledge and understanding of the world and creative development (Foundation Stage Curriculum). Through this work children can begin to develop knowledge and understanding of the different sounds made by the instruments and the three main characteristics of sound; loudness, pitch and quality or timbre. At this age children are likely to think that big objects make loud sounds and small objects quiet sounds, and the idea that loudness is measured by the pressure it makes on the ear drum is clearly not one held. They should begin to recognize if the instrument makes a loud or quiet sound or a high or low one and they can try to explain how they make different notes on different instruments. Children can also develop their ability to recognize the sounds made by different instruments (the timbre or quality of the sound) by exploring, identifying and explaining how the different sounds are made. In science, children in the Foundation Stage of Learning can explore the instruments and find out some features of them, such as pitch, loudness, recognition (K&U4 or Knowledge and Understanding Early Learning Goal 4). At Key Stage 1 they can explore the different ways the instruments make sounds (plucking, banging, blowing, shaking) and try making the instruments make higher, lower, louder or quieter sounds (Sc4 or Science Attainment Target 4, see Table 1.2).

They will also develop technologic knowledge and understanding of the use of tools to make the instruments (K&U8) and vocabulary related to the concept of sound (high, low, sound, quiet, loud, pitch, noise, music, etc.).

Summary

- Learning theories have helped us to understand that children develop understanding of the world through exploration and investigation.
- Factors affecting the development of knowledge and understanding include prior experiences, language development, practitioners' own knowledge and the quality of interaction during explorations.
- Children's thinking skills in science can be enhanced through quality interaction.
- Through exploration, children will develop knowledge and understanding in different areas of knowledge in a holistic way.

4

Developing positive attitudes in science

When young children are playing, they are often able to solve simple problems by trial and error. Early toys encourage them to press buttons, fit objects into slots and generally explore a variety of phenomena. In doing this, children are not only developing ideas about the world around them, they are also developing useful skills for future scientific development. They are learning to look, to feel, to predict. Additionally, they are developing useful attitudes such as curiosity and perseverance. They will often sit for considerable periods of time trying to perform a task such as putting shapes into shaped slots. Once they have achieved this they will repeat it again and again. They are obviously motivated by the need to succeed. Attitudes such as curiosity and perseverance are essential in science and other areas of learning to enable children to maximize learning and develop ideas and skills. In this way children are developing their attitudes alongside their skills and understandings through informal and formal science experiences. Therefore, the model described in Chapter 2 (Figure 2.2) needs enlarging to encompass attitudes. If the experiences they have are motivating and inspire children with awe and wonder, then they are more likely to develop skills and understandings and they will also develop an intrinsic desire to continue learning.

Figure 4.1   The development of scientific conceptual understanding skills and attitudes

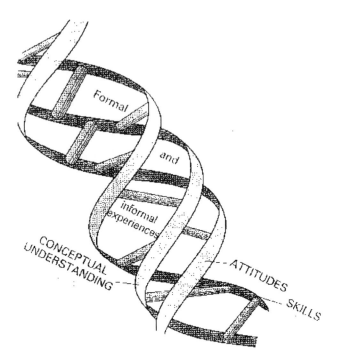

The area of attitudes is complex and it overlaps with all aspects of life. An attitude can be described as a 'posture or position that is adopted' or an 'expression of a view or thought' (*Chambers Twentieth Century Dictionary*). Attitudes can usually be observed in some kind of behaviour and the importance of the resulting behaviours is thought to affect development, in general, in the early years in general (QCA, 2000) and specifically in science in all stages of learning (DfEE, 1999; Bricheno *et al.*, 2000). The development of scientific attitudes has been an important part of school science for many years. The early development of the National Curriculum acknowledged the importance of scientific attitudes (DES, 1987) but identified difficulties in their assessment (DES, 1987; 1988). The result was that in the eyes of many teachers attitudes were devalued. If we do not have to assess them, why should we develop them? Their recognition as important developmental aspects is recognized in the Foundation Curriculum (QCA, 2000), but appears forgotten in a curriculum-focused Key Stage 1 with an emphasis on national targets in literacy and numeracy.

Arguments for the development of attitudes are twofold: that we should be developing the whole child and that the development of positive attitudes is likely to have an important effect on the development of scientific concepts, knowledge and skills. The development of positive attitudes is important for effective learning, not only because the attitudes we possess affect our behaviour and development, but also because they affect the way we feel about science. Affective attitudes, or the way we feel, is thought to be 'the root of both cognitive and behavioural attitudes, so that how we behave is a result of how we think and an inter-relation of how we feel and think' (Bricheno *et al.*, 2000: 143). Concerns about current educational practice in Key Stages 1 and 2 and the effect on emotional and social development, including attitudes, have led some schools to teach the curriculum through the six key areas of learning of the Foundation Stage curriculum. Time and research will show how effective this approach is in redressing the balance in the curriculum.

Scientific attitudes

There are a number of attitudes which we should develop as part of the education process. Many are generic attitudes, needed throughout education and in social or work contexts later in life (for example, co-operation and perseverance). Some of these attitudes are specifically important in science teaching and learning (for example respect for evidence and tentativeness) and need to be developed throughout formal and informal learning. Some of these attitudes are affective or emotional (for example, enthusiasm), others are cognitive (for example, curiosity, respect for evidence, thoughtfulness, reflection, tentativeness, question-ing) and others are social or behavioural (such as co-operation, collaboration, tolerance, flexibility, independence, perseverance, leader-ship, responsibility, tenaciousness). For the purposes of science education, these attitudes can be assigned broad groupings and there is some overlap between them (Figure 4.2).

Many of the attitudes we would wish to develop in children are useful to other areas of learning as well as later in life. We would wish children to be co-operative, tolerant, flexible and sensitive in many aspects of their education and wider learning outside school. The young egocentric child described in Chapter 1 will not readily be co-operative or flexible. Indeed, the development of these attitudes is similar to the development of concepts and skills, in that it is a long process. As with skills and concepts we need to have an overview of the attitudes needed for successful development and we need to work continually towards the development of those attitudes. Children in our care will not develop fully in this area

Figure 4.2   A model for the development of scientific attitudes

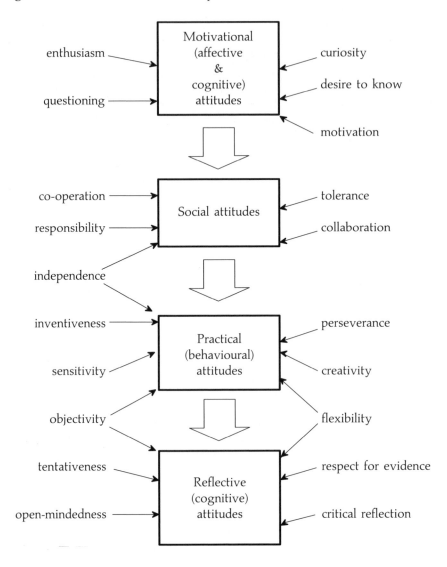

but our teaching should provide the foundations for the development of positive attitudes throughout their future lives.

Motivating attitudes

These are the attitudes that are necessary in the initiation of and throughout an exploration. In order for children to develop and learn about the world around them and scientific phenomena, they need to be motivated. Motivating attitudes affect the way a child feels and behaves and so are affective and cognitive. We see the effects of motivating attitudes in curious, questioning children, who are enthusiastic about exploring the world around them. Without enthusiasm, interest or the drive to want to find out or know about something, learning will be less effective and teaching becomes an impossible task. As teachers we have an important role in encouraging children's explorations, and in order to be successful in this we need to understand how a child develops the desire to learn. All children show some curiosity and, if encouraged, this will develop into a motivation to learn about the world around them. Sometimes this curiosity is discouraged, particularly where it could lead the child into danger. The present generation of children have fewer opportunities to be adventurous than previous generations. This is connected to the complexities and dangers of today's society. As a young child I was not particularly adventurous, but spent a great deal of time exploring my environment and discovering the delights of the local woods, waste-land and building sites and, in doing so, developed scientific knowledge which was useful in my future life. Today children's lives are more structured. Parents today generally do not consider it safe for young children to frequent building sites; we are concerned about the safety of our children when 'playing out' and we tend to keep a much closer eye on our children than parents of former years. In some respects, children have paid for this greater care and have fewer opportunities for free play and exploration. While this picture of middle-class life does not ring true for all of the children of today, the basic tenet remains that children have less opportunity for developing curiosity. For many children the instinctive need to find out is thwarted because it is not always convenient to have a child constantly asking questions, touching things and enquiring. Take a class full of inquisitive three- or five-year-old children and it is necessary to channel their inquisitiveness, not only because of safety but because they should learn to consider the needs of others.

Learning that they are not the centre of the universe is a hard lesson for all children and the consequences are often that their desire to find out, to learn, is damaged. Donaldson (1978) describes this in terms of a tension between wanting to know and the process of finding out. Very young children have no ability to see the consequences of their actions, and as the ability to think inwardly about actions develops and children are able to deduce from inference what will happen, they will often appear less curious even if they are not less curious. Their decision not to find out may be based on experience: 'I won't explore the pond because I've fallen in three times or because my parents have told me off three times.' It may be that they decide not to explore because they expect a certain outcome, even if it is not based on experience. They may have been told something will happen or be able to imagine it happening. Children who will not go near a snake have probably not been bitten by one; they may not have been told that snakes bite, but they have developed their ideas from a variety of sources which will influence their curiosity about snakes. At one time, my son was terrified of fireworks. He was convinced that one would land on his head. This was not because one had hurt him or because he had been told they would land on his head, but because he deduced 'that what goes up must come down and it will probably be on my head'.

Curiosity is perhaps the most important attitude for exploration. Curious children have the need to know about everything they interact with, and this leads to the ability to raise questions and to investigate. Not all children display curiosity, and this needs to be encouraged in school if children are to benefit fully from their explorations. Harlen (1977b) has identified four possible causes for a lack of curiosity in children: temperament, experience, environment and social constraints. These factors interact to make the identification of causes difficult. Quiet children in an unfamiliar context, newly arrived in school and with low self-confidence, may appear to be lacking in curiosity but it may be that their reserve hides their interest. Similarly, children whose previous experiences have discouraged them from exploring or who have previously had their over-zealous curiosity suppressed may not choose to be curious or, at least, overtly curious. While very young children can spend long periods of time exploring (see Chapter 1), as the world opens up to them children will be attracted to new situations. In the midst of so many new experiences their curiosity is often short-lived and they quickly move on to the next situation. As they develop, their interest will be sustained for longer periods of time and they make use of all their senses, and it is often at this stage that a multitude of questions are raised that are seemingly impossible to answer or investigate. Further development leads to detailed observations and the need to understand.

When introducing new experiences into a Key Stage 1 classroom I have been met with exclamations of 'Ooo, what is it?', 'Is it a . . . ?', 'Do they ... ?', 'Can we ... ?' and even 'What do we do with it?' and 'What does it do?' In addition, a mass of hands are wanting to delve in and explore. This is not, however, the situation for all children in the class. There are always some who appear not to show an interest or choose not to explore or who, during carpet-time discussions, sit quietly waiting for the end. Children should be encouraged to display curiosity, by being encouraged to observe closely, explore and raise questions. For this to occur satisfactorily, time needs to be set aside for quality exploration of a range of different phenomena. These can be from within the children's experience, where they are able to look at the familiar in a different way, or new phenomena, the exploration of which may need encouragement for less confident children. Once children are curious enough to explore and are able to listen to the ideas of others, knowing they are valued, they will become more open-minded and tolerant and will feel more confident about expressing their ideas.

We need to harness natural curiosity and help children to develop the desire to learn within the parameters we set them, and this is where other attitudes overlap with curiosity. Motivational attitudes are important generic attitudes, needed in all areas of learning. Another set of generic attitudes are social ones, needed when children mix with their peers in work and play.

Social attitudes

Children need to consider the needs and safety of others. Within their families they soon learn that other children and adults have needs and rights. When they mix with larger numbers of children in play schools, nurseries and at school, this need to consider others becomes more important. They cannot rush around and explore everything they want, when they want. They have to conform to school rules. Sometimes this is difficult for children and it creates a conflict between school and the child. In the worst situation alienation occurs and children resent having to be at school and having to conform.

Regardless of the way we organize the scientific experiences, play situations, collaborative, co-operative group work, individual explorations or even whole-class demonstrations, we expect children to be able to work with or alongside others. Play can be useful in supporting social development (Bruner *et al.*, 1976). In the early years children will often engage in parallel play, that is, play alongside each other before they begin to play co-operatively and Moyles (1989) argues that most educational settings provide play opportunities which encourage parallel rather than co-operative play. Lindon (2001) believes that young children can and do play together, but that older children are often more engaged in parallel play, possibly, as Moyles argues (1989), because the opportunities for true co-operation and collaboration are limited. As they move into Key Stage 1, science explorations may be more directed and the children may be expected to work in groups, although this is often more individual work undertaken alongside others. It is only later that they are able to work collaboratively. Indeed, even older children engaged in scientific activities may 'learn more efficiently when working individually rather than with others' (Harlen, 1977b: 27). However, the sharing of ideas and efforts can provide very effective learning opportunities and should be encouraged where appropriate. We need fully to consider the attitudes and skills needed for effective group participation. I am not convinced that we, as adults, are particularly good at group work. If this is so, then it becomes all the more important that we consider what attitudes and skills are needed and plan how these can be developed in both ourselves and those we teach.

In order to work effectively as a group, or individually within a group, children need to co-operate with each other. We know that children are capable of co-operation at a young age (Lindon, 2001), but that their ability to co-operate will depend on the opportunities provided for social development and also adult interaction (Bennett *et al.*, 1997). Co-operation should occur regardless of the group's members – whether the group is based on friendship, gender, ability or any other criteria. Practitioners may attempt to group children according to different criteria or allow them to group themselves, but the long-term aim must be to enable children to work in any group regardless of the group constitution. Children who are fully co-operative in a group situation will be responsive to the needs of others in the group, will try to accommodate the ideas of others and will settle group difficulties without resorting to argument or appeal to the teacher. Young children are not naturally co-operative; indeed they are more likely to be competitive (Dean, 2001) or to work independently in group situations. They are often reluctant to share resources or ideas with others and the group may need constant supervision to avoid disputes occurring. In some cases competition can work against co-operation (Dean, 2001), although with sensitive interaction competition can be challenging and motivating, especially where the children are not competing against each other and the level of challenge is appropriate. The practitioner may need to interact with the children to organize them and model co-operative behaviours. As the children become more used to working together, the practitioner will need to lay down a set of rules for working in groups and will then need to wean children off teacher support and encourage them to make up their own rules for working. For this to occur there needs to be adequate time provided to allow the children to 'sort themselves out', to make group decisions, and this should be built into any working plans. Children thus supported in co-operative work should be able to begin to work collaboratively on an activity towards a common goal.

When working in group situations children need to be tolerant towards other group members. They need to consider the needs of all the group and respect the ideas of others. This may mean initially selecting groups which are able to co-operate with each other. These groups should not remain static. Membership and roles (co-ordinating the group, recording decisions, and so on) should change from time to time to enable children to learn and display scientific attitudes in a variety of situations.

Working in groups makes science activities organizationally easier than individual work, but in many instances children at this age work individually within a group. I observed one mixed group of children who were working together, in a competitive situation, making paper aeroplanes. The task was to make an aeroplane which would fly over 10 metres. For each aeroplane that achieved this the team would get a point. The group divided into gender sub-groups, with the boys quickly making successful aeroplanes but not wishing to help the girls, who were uncertain how to design an aeroplane. The fact that the girls' inability to make a successful aeroplane would mean fewer points for the whole team was immaterial! Even with young children gender issues play an important part in inhibiting good attitudes for group participation. It is clear that, whatever the group constitution, co-operation is not a natural part of human behaviour. Team work in adults is often little better. We can democratically make decisions, but individuals often interpret these differently or ignore them and follow their own course. If we do not always see attitudes for group participation in older children and even in adults, it is very unlikely that Foundation and Key Stage 1 children will exhibit better-developed attitudes. These attitudes need to be continually encouraged, throughout the learning process, in order for their development to be successful.

Mixed-ability grouping can also cause difficulties in investigations. These groups often consist of individuals with different attitudes in and attitudes to science, as well as different abilities (Johnston, 1992; Bricheno *et al.*, 2000). In such instances the investigation can enhance rather than dissipate anxieties. This is because more advanced learners can be so enthused with their own hypotheses that the insecure are carried along and do not have the opportunity to explore their ideas and develop at their own rate. Sometimes co-operation and competition become confused, as it did with the group of children described earlier. However, ability grouping in science is not usually feasible because ability in science tends to differ from concept to concept and children are usually assigned to ability groups on the basis of language development rather than science.

Children have all experienced being compared to others, even before they come to school, and they quite easily interpret what we consider to be co-operation to mean competition. Some children are so anxious not to fail that they will not compete or even co-operate. To a young child, failure means frustration and unhappiness, and success in a competitive situation is not available to all.

Responsibility is another important attitude for both individual and group work. Children who take full responsibility for their learning are able to work independently, without constant supervision, and will attempt to overcome problems they face without teacher help. Young children will need considerable help to reach this stage in their development as it presupposes a maturity and experience lacking in young children, but with help and guidance they can begin to play a more responsible part in their own learning. Piaget (1929; 1950) and Kohlberg (1976) identify a close relationship between the development of responsibility and cognitive development, with children in the early years. In Piaget's sensori-motor stages of development, or Kohlberg's pre-conventional stage of morality, children will be unaware of the needs of others. As they develop socially and morally they are firstly idiosyncratic in their responsibility and application of social rules (Piaget's pre-operational stage of development). Then they apply rules rigorously (Piaget's concrete operational stage and Kohlberg's conventional stage of morality). Understanding these stages does not mean that we can expect responsibility to develop without opportunity. We need to provide children with a framework in which they can take responsibility for their own development and also to provide time for them to make decisions for themselves and resolve any difficulties. They also need good role models from which to imitate and develop their own ideas of responsibility. They should develop the understanding that they are responsible for their own actions. It is a natural human reaction to rationalize why things do not go according to plan but it is not enough to deny responsibility because intention is absent. Steven, a Year 2 child, had a wonderful experience exploring materials but there was considerable mess on the floor. When asked to tidy it up he responded 'It's not my fault, I didn't mean to.' This kind of response is becoming more apparent in all ages of learners, from children through to adults, and we need to develop the idea that responsibility does not mean blame and that we can be responsible for our scientific explorations without blame when things go wrong. Without this knowledge children are unlikely to want to be either responsible or inventive as it could lead to trouble.

We would want all children to develop attitudes to assist group participation – co-operation, tolerance, responsibility and leadership – but we should remember that they do not exist naturally. We should also remember that being a member of a group is not easy for children and should attempt to develop these attitudes in a coherent way.

Practical attitudes

There are some important attitudes necessary, or desirable, for effective engagement in an exploration or investigation. These are mainly behavioural in nature and can be seen through the behaviour of children. One such attitude is creativity, which is recognized (Beetlestone, 1998; QCA, 2000) as an important attitude associated with learning. Our understanding of creativity in learning is often limited to art, music and design, although Beetlestone's (1998) six-part definition of creativity as a form of,

- learning
- representation
- productivity
- originality
- thinking creatively/problem-solving
- universe/creation-nature

has provided us with a broader understanding appropriate to science. Therefore, creativity involves an interrelationship between 'skills, emotional responses, imagination, making connections and taking risks' (Compton, 2002: 194) or in early-years science specifically hypothetical or creative intuitive thinking (de Bóo, 1999). That creativity is important for children in their scientific explorations comes as a surprise to some in society, because their image of science is not compatible with the broader notion of creativity. Another problem in developing creative attitudes in young children is that there is little guidance on how we develop children's creativity. Children learn from us what aspects we value and, in many cases, creativity in science is not one of them. We need to remember that creative scientists are the key to the future, and we should encourage all our future scientists in their creativity. Planning creative experiences for creative thinking is discussed further in Chapter 6. The message about the nature of science, as being cold, unimaginative and uncreative, seems to contradict children's drawings of scientists which often include evidence of imaginative thought and new creative ideas through the inclusion of Eureka bubbles and light bulbs (Figure 4.3; see also Chambers, 1983). As practitioners, we need to develop in children positive scientific attitudes, along with an understanding of scientific concepts, the skills of science and the nature of science and to ensure they see the creative side of scientific exploration.

Within the scientific process children also need to exhibit flexibility and independence. This is different from flexibility of thought, which will be discussed later in the chapter. Flexibility in the process of science involves children in being prepared to modify or abandon their line of exploration or investigation because a more fruitful one emerges. This flexibility is also an essential ingredient in working with others in an exploration as children need to be flexible enough to encompass the views of others. Independence involves children in having ideas of their own about the exploration they are involved in and this is highly valued by teachers (Bennett *et al.*, 1997) for pragmatic reasons as well as because it is of value in future life. The development of independence involves children in moving away from the automatic acceptance of others' ideas and being able to make decisions for themselves. Like co-operation, independence does not come naturally to children (Dean, 2001) and a structured approach is best. These decisions should be based on all the available evidence and not be made just because someone else has a similar idea. Children need to have the confidence, responsibility and independence to explore and investigate in and beyond the classroom, and to approach and use other sources of information such as outside agencies and experts.

While exploring and investigating, children need perseverance. They should not give up at the first attempt if something does not succeed. Early perseverance in children can be described as 'the tendency to continue an activity or task once it has begun, despite difficulties or lack of immediate success' (Harlen, 1977a: 36). We all recognize the young child who says 'I can't do it', having made little or no attempt at the task. As children develop they are more likely to persevere with activities regardless of the effort involved providing there is a reasonable chance of success. They are also more likely to try other ways of working in order to achieve a successful result. The types of activity we give to children and the way we structure activities can help to develop perseverance in children. Activities should not be so difficult that children cannot see a way forward and give up. Children need to feel a degree of success and a sense of achievement in order to motivate them further, that is develop positive attitudes and dispositions towards learning (QCA, 2000). When they do encounter difficulties in their explorations they need help in identifying the way forward and encouragement to persevere.

Objectivity is a very important attitude in science because without it the development of scientific skills, concepts and knowledge is impaired. Objectivity is implicit in many parts of the scientific process. It is the basis of fair testing and, as described in Chapter 2, it can be developed through explorations. Successful interpretation of data requires a degree of objectivity to enable unbiased interpretations to occur. Objectivity is necessary in order for children to identify variables and undertake fair testing. Raper and Stringer (1987) believe that fair testing will help to develop both objectivity and honesty. There is a cognitive component to objectivity and fair testing (de Bóo, 1999) and children are unlikely to be able to be fully objective in the early years. We can support children in the skill of fair testing and the attitude of objectivity by encouraging them in examination of their ideas and practice and valuing their failures as stepping-stones to success.

Within an exploration or investigation sensitivity towards others is necessary (QCA, 2000). This includes sensitivity towards the views and abilities of other children but also sensitivity towards, and a responsibility for, all living things in the environment. 'Unless investigation and exploration are governed by an attitude of respect for the environment and a willingness to care appropriately for the living things in it, such activities could result in unnecessary interference or unpleasant harm' (Harlen, 2000: 79). These attitudes develop mainly through example. Good examples come from teachers who develop an understanding of the world around them by observing animals and plants in their natural environment or creating suitable environments in the classroom. It is possible to study plants and animals in the school, but we need to be careful that we understand all the needs of those plants and animals to enable us to care adequately for them. We should not collect plants and animals and study them in school unless we are able to return them to their natural environment later. If we collect frog spawn from a local pond and neglect the needs of the developing frogs the result will be a smelly, messy death for the animals concerned, and children will not pick up the positive messages about the importance of caring for living things.

We also need to be careful that we do not encourage anthropomorphism. Animals and plants have different needs than ours, and we cannot assign human values when dealing with them. What is considered bliss for a wood-louse, rotting wood, vegetation and darkness, is considered abhorrent to us. I have been involved in creating wildlife areas within school where children can attract butterflies, explore pond life and grow wild flowers. I have also provided a safe environment for other animals to live in school. At one school we kept rabbits in a school quad, where they could roam freely during the day and be observed and cared for by the children. We also used an incubator to hatch ducklings who later went to live at another teacher's home. The development of understanding and sensitivity towards living things engendered by these activities was great. On another occasion children were involved in planting trees and shrubs on some waste land. In doing this they developed an understanding of the need for these plants, both aesthetically and physically. In taking responsibility for the planting the children were also less likely to destroy the trees and shrubs at a later date and to dissuade others from doing so.

We can also provide a good example by the way in which we conduct ourselves inside or outside the classroom. Swatting flies and ignoring litter are bad examples. Releasing flies and spiders back into the outside world and picking up litter are good examples. One teacher I know always carries a plastic bag around with her to pick up any pieces of litter left by others. This has had an effect on children around her who become much more aware of the mess around them and more willing to dispose of not only their own waste but also of others' waste.

Reflective attitudes

Reflective attitudes are mainly cognitive in nature and involve the child in developing their thinking skills and can aid the development of knowledge and understanding. In undertaking an exploration or investigation children need to develop reflective attitudes. These are attitudes which help them objectively to consider their data, interpret evidence and make tentative hypotheses, but remain flexible enough to change their ideas if they are not consistent with the evidence. Children need to embark on a scientific activity with an open mind; this involves considering the views of others but not, of course, total acceptance of others' ideas without due consideration of their own. Young children will often have firm ideas about phenomena based on their own experience, but because their experiences are limited their ideas may be unsophisticated. They may also, in some cases, be so firmly held that they inhibit the process of exploration and investigation (Driver, 1983; Johnston, 2002a). Ideas, while firmly held, may also be hidden. This may be because the ideas of others, particularly the teacher, are respected and are not contradicted. This indicates some degree of tolerance on the children's part, and while we would wish them to tolerate the ideas and interpretations of others they do need to have the ability and confidence to challenge ideas and interpretations if they do not match their own. In some respects children seem able to allow two contradictory ideas to exist together and often do not appear to recognize that they are contradictory (Driver *et al.*, 1985).

Having obtained evidence which either confirms or contradicts their ideas, children then need to have respect for that evidence. Harlen (2000: 78) identifies respect for evidence as 'being central to scientific activity'. Respecting evidence implies that the children are not biased in their interpretations because of existing ideas. They need to realize that if the evidence does not match their ideas and expectations they may challenge the evidence but not ignore it. They still need to respect valid interpretations based on the evidence which are not compatible with their ideas and expectations. There is an element of tentativeness involved in respecting evidence. Children need to see that all evidence is tentative, that they can only draw conclusions with supporting evidence, and that, even then, the conclusions may be subject to challenge.

Children also need to be flexible enough to change their ideas in the light of evidence or to review procedures critically (Harlen and Jelly, 1997). Flexibility involves a recognition that there may be other ways of looking at evidence, a willingness to consider evidence from alternative viewpoints and to change ideas in the light of evidence. To reflect critically on a scientific exploration or investigation involves a willingness to consider alternative ways of undertaking an investigation to improve the outcome – to evaluate procedure. This often involves consideration of how an investigation was best suited to answer questions raised during initial exploration. It could involve consideration of the planning of an investigation or how 'fair' the investigation was. As Harlen (2000) has indicated, this is a mature activity and young children find it difficult. As children develop, their ability to think critically develops and becomes more organized, 'rational, creative and critical' (de Bóo, 1999: 77), as they are supported by practitioners. Sharing ideas, planning and interpretations helps to identify different perspectives and has the initial advantage of giving children access to the ideas of others. Development of group co-operation skills and consideration for others assist in the further development of these attitudes.

The development of all attitudes in science is a long process. Like the development of skills and concepts, children will progress at a rate compatible with their abilities. The analogy with building a wall is apt. The final wall is our aim and although we may only lay a few bricks we need to understand the final wall plan, know what mix of cement to use and what size bricks are best. In the development of young children we only lay a few bricks, but they are the foundation for a wall which will be very robust. We need to have a clear idea of children's developmental needs and how they might progress. We need to know what scientific attitudes are necessary for children to develop and how those attitudes can be developed. This knowledge will enable us to assist children's development effectively.

The development of attitudes in the classroom

A class of Year 3 children engaged in scientific exploration and investigation of 'air' illustrated for me the complex nature of attitude development and the many influences on it. These children were involved in exploring a range of scientific ideas including the idea that air had *weight* (scientifically this should be mass). This idea had been introduced to them and they had accepted it and were undertaking explorations and investigations to illustrate it. They were working in small groups and were extremely motivated, enthusiastically debating ideas and questioning each other about their ideas. Within the groups there was considerable evidence of co-operation as well as tolerance of others' ideas.

One investigation to illustrate that 'air had weight' was to balance a stick, on a pencil, on top of a tin or on a finger. The fulcrum point on the stick was marked with a pencil (Picture 4.1). Two balloons were attached to the ends of the sticks and the balance point checked. Then one balloon was blown up and reattached. The children predicted that the inflated balloon would 'go down' and their hypothesis for this was 'because air has weight'. When their predicted outcome occurred the children were confused and unhappy even though they had predicted correctly. One child said 'I've got the mark in the wrong place' and proceeded to change the pencil mark, indicating the point of balance, until the inflated balloon

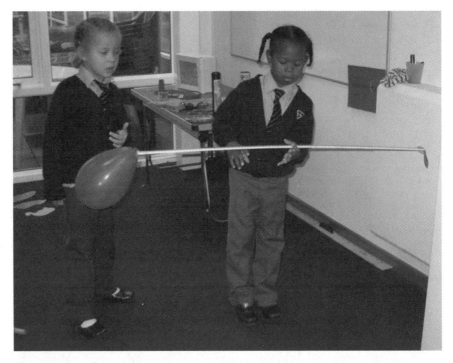

Picture 4.1 *Investigating whether air has* weight *(sic)*

rose into the air. Another child said 'We've done it wrong' and even though he had written down his prediction he then finished his recording with an explanation as to what he thought should have happened.

These children had accepted the teacher's idea that air had weight, even though they had no evidence to support it and it contradicted their own ideas, that air was light or weightless. They were fully involved in the investigative procedure, but they had not planned the investigation out of their own explorations and observations and in answer to their own questions. During the activity they demonstrated good development of motivating attitudes, social attitudes and, to a lesser extent, practical attitudes. The development of their reflective attitudes was very uncertain. They had firmly held ideas which contradicted the ideas of the teacher and, while they tolerated her ideas, they did not consider them in the final interpretation. They did not respect the evidence from their investigation when it challenged their ideas. It never occurred to them that the results could indicate that their ideas about 'light air', which led them to believe that the inflated balloon would rise, were incorrect. They were not flexible in their ideas and neither were they able to reflect critically on the investigation and see if the investigation was the cause for a discrepancy in their ideas and findings.

The classroom activity surrounding this work on air also illustrated an important factor affecting the development of children's scientific development. During all the scientific explorations and investigations the children were obviously motivated, enthusiastic and curious. Some activities were very experiential and exploratory, while others, like the one described above, were more structured and had an expected outcome. I was very impressed with the children's involvement. At the end of a week of intense activity and development the children were asked to review their week and indicate what learning they had enjoyed and what learning they had disliked. Science did not fare very well during this evaluation. They had fun during the science activities but they did not like them. They did not like exploratory activities. They liked activities where a 'correct' answer resulted. They wanted assurances that they were progressing well, and science did not give them such assurances. Neither did they like activities that challenged their existing ideas. They wanted safety and confidence. They found this in a page of mathematical calculations which received a page of red ticks. This story illustrates the effect on scientific learning of the 'hidden curriculum' which is present in every school. Children, teachers and parents often have different views of education, different aims and different learning preferences and these can adversely affect the development of the child.

We all have different teaching and learning preferences (Johnston, 1996, see Chapter 6). These preferences reflect the way all involved with the school view learning and form part of the learning milieu or school ethos, influencing both our attitudes to science as well as the choice of teaching and learning methods used by the teachers we encounter. The choice of teaching and learning method will actually form part of the total experience in science for learners and sends powerful messages about the nature of science.

Attitudes to science

Affective attitudes will determine the way we feel about scientific activity. However, one difficulty concerning attitudes towards science is that they are not regarded as a single construct (Simon, 2000), although there have been successful attempts to define them. Fraser (1981) identified seven separate constructs which together contribute towards an overall attitude to science. These are attitudes

- towards the social implications of science;
- towards the normality of scientists;
- to scientific enquiry;
- needed to be scientific;
- towards the enjoyment of science;
- towards science as a leisure interest;
- towards a career in science.

Generally, children have been found (Simon, 2000; Bricheno *et al.*, 2000) to have a positive attitude towards science, although this may not positively affect their choices for further study and their attitudes later in life. We need continually to develop positive affective attitudes so that children have a positive image of science. The reasons why we need to do this can be considered from three different viewpoints: the viewpoint of the individual; the viewpoint of society; and the viewpoint of science and scientists.

Children as individuals need to have a positive image of science. By this I mean a full and accurate picture of the nature and different aspects of science. They need this positive image, not to coerce them into science as a career but to allow them to make an informed decision as to whether science has a part to play in their general lives. Many adults, let alone children, are unaware that they use scientific skills and knowledge in many aspects of their lives; when adapting mixtures when baking, choosing a diet for healthy living and weight loss, or mending a broken electrical toy. A full and accurate picture of science can assist children and adults in important decision-making, and without it understanding and interpretation of scientific issues within society are difficult (Millar and Wynne, 1988). These may be decisions that affect our immediate environment and the planet as a whole. For example, a full understanding of how science influences the environment allows us to make personal, local and national decisions, such as why we should recycle resources, why the local community needs a bypass and what the national government's policy on the disposal of hazardous waste should involve. An understanding of genetics and medical science allows us to make informed decisions as to the ethics and desirability of genetic engineering or whether we should vaccinate our children using a triple vaccine. Without the knowledge we are not in a position to make these decisions. This knowledge directly influences the attitudes we have about science. If our attitudes are based on accurate knowledge they are more likely to be positive than if based on hearsay and innuendo. However, research (Irwin and Wynne, 1996; Miller *et al.*, 1997) indicates that scientific literacy is not common in society and is an extremely complex concept, although many adults are extremely competent on a need-to-know basis. Schools are also not very competent in developing positive understanding of the nature of science (Jenkins, 2000) and there is a significant decline in attitudes during secondary schooling (Yager and Penick, 1986; Doherty and Dawe, 1988; Bricheno *et al.*, 2000). This may reflect the declining interest and familiarity of content from concrete aspects of the world such as living things, natural phenomena and familiar technology to more abstract scientific phenomena set in unfamiliar contexts, such as gravitational force, electricity and acoustics.

Positive attitudes to science are also important to society. Western society is dependent on commercial and scientific endeavours and this has emphasized the need for greater scientific understanding to further good scientific and technological development. Greater scientific understanding will enable society to understand the effect of science, technology and industry on our environment and empower us as a society to make ecological decisions. The popularization of science and the drive for relevant science for society in the last few decades has not necessarily had a significant effect on attitudes to science (Fensham, 2001) and views of science in society. There is also a need for good science graduates, equipped with relevant knowledge and skills, to further scientific and technological advances. There is concern that few young people who study science at school continue to study science at a higher level (Sears, 1995) or follow science career pathways (Millar and Wynne, 1988). Enthusiasm for science appears to be dwindling and there is evidence (Bricheno *et al.*, 2000) that this is nothing to do with the popularity of science education, but due in part to the perception that science and technology will not aid successful future careers, particularly with respect to financial status. It may be a self-perpetuating cycle. Successful heads of industry are not scientists and therefore science is not the vehicle for success in industry. However, Jenkins (2000) identifies a dilemma that skills-based science faces; are we engaged in training future scientists for our industrialized society or are we educating future citizens by developing their intellectual and moral thinking as citizens in a democratic society? It may be, as Chapman (1991) has indicated, that a post-industrial society with diminishing employment for future generations will not need the emphasis we place on science in the National Curriculum – that is, unless we focus on the political and economic issues surrounding science to enable us as individuals and society to make important decisions with a global, national and individual perspective.

From the viewpoint of science and scientists, it is important to develop positive attitudes to science, to dispel the misconception that science is only appropriate for scientists. The mythical scientists are that strange breed of 'men', intelligent, grey-haired, bespectacled, eccentric, with test tubes or leaky pens in their pockets and a bemused expression on their faces, who muck up the environment (Harlen, 2000; Figure 4.3). We only need to look as far as young children's pictures of scientists (Chambers, 1983) to see evidence of this image and to realize that it is not surprising that they do not see themselves as scientists. Changes in the stereotypical view are slow, although there is some evidence (Matthews, 1996) to indicate that the image children have of scientists is slowly becoming more realistically normal.

Providing good role models in school and illustrating the differing parts played by science in society will help to change the stereotyped view of science and the scientist. I would like children to be aware of the multifaceted, creative and qualitative aspects of science and to see its

Figure 4.3   A child's picture of a scientist

value in the widest sense, not, as I stated earlier, to coerce them into science as a career but to make them aware of its true nature and to decide for themselves the part it has to play in their lives.

As individuals we need to ask ourselves the question 'What is science?' We also need to help children to begin to answer the same question. The ideas people have about science can be divided into five categories, reflected in the following questions:

- Can science be *qualitative* in nature, or is it always *quantitative*?
- Is science *impersonal* or *personal*?
- Is it necessary always to be *objective* in science, or is there room to be *subjective*?
- Can science teaching accommodate differing views, that is, is it *value-free* or *value-dependent*?
- Does science carry its own *moral* code, or is it *amoral*?

Young children will have their own answers to a similar set of questions which will help to build up a picture of their attitudes to science:

- Who is a scientist?
- What do scientists do?
- Do scientists care for people, animals, plants?
- Can science help us?

Attitudes to science are affected by a number of influences in our lives (Figure 4.4).

Figure 4.4   Factors affecting attitudes

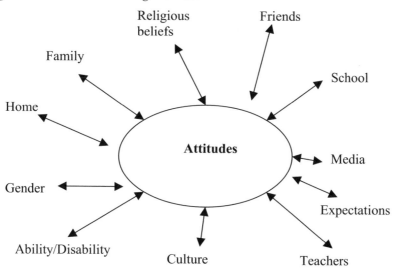

Home and Family

The home and family are major influences on the development of children's attitudes to science. Children's attitudes to science are formed as a result of influences before they arrive in school (Smail, 1984), earlier than 'most other subjects' (Harlen, 1985: 5), which indicates the profound influence of parents. The importance of parental attitudes and home–school partnership is recognized as of great importance (ASE, 1993; QCA, 2000; Siraj-Blatchford *et al.* 2002; DfES, 2003) as is the provision of information to parents and school governors so that they develop a greater understanding of the investigative process and science itself. Sometimes science can appear to alienate itself from the average parent because of scientific language. Sometimes scientists hold different notions about the world or assign different meanings to words. There are differences in the meaning of the word 'science' (Johnston *et al.*, 1998) as a result of differences in experiences. If home and school science experiences focus on one area of science, then this will predominate when thinking about science in later life. Environmental experiences may lead to an understanding of science that emphasizes the environment. Some school science experiences may lead to an understanding that science is only practical in nature or emphasize process skills above conceptual development. The language of science can send messages which will help to develop views of science (see also Chapter 3 and Johnston, 2003). There are differences in the meanings of words such as 'force' and 'energy' which have a common usage as well as a scientific usage. Ideas about the meanings of words such as 'exploratory' and 'practical' may differ in meaning or scope. The most worrying perception that parents can hold is that science, while important, has no part to play in their lives. There appear to be many families who feel that science is not applicable to their lives and there is a gap between the perceptions that parents have of science and the part that science plays in individual lives. A parent who makes wine at home may understand the wine-making process but believe he/she understands little or no chemistry. A keen gardener can be an amateur ecologist and have a good understanding of the environment. A snooker player must be able to understand forces and their effects. A dog breeder must have some understanding of genetics. If we are removing stains from clothes we must be able to identify which soap powders are the most effective and understand something about materials and their properties. Science plays an important part in all our lives. To provide a coherent understanding of science we need to be aware of this and of the full nature of science.

School and teachers

The attitudes towards science held outside school are likely to be mirrored in school and these can include rather narrow views of science and scientists, as I have indicated earlier (Irwin and Wynne, 1996; Miller *et al.*, 1997). The methods of teaching and learning in each area of knowledge send powerful messages about the knowledge itself. Is it difficult, boring, fun or interactive? Is it incomprehensible, logical or intuitive? The way in which we teach science, our knowledge of teaching strategies, common pupil conceptions and learning difficulties, otherwise known as pedagogical content knowledge (De Jong, 2003), can affect the children's attitudes towards science (Woolnough, 1994; Hendley *et al.*, 1995) and the kind of science teaching experienced has been found (Haladyna *et al.*, 1982) to be the most important factor in pupil attitude towards science. Choices about teaching and learning methods are often made as a result of considerations such as organization, teachers' knowledge and background and the National Curriculum programmes of study.

During science play and exploration, interaction between the teacher and the child occurs and through this an adult will, often unconsciously, influence developing attitudes. The development of attitudes to science can be influenced by the adult's own prejudices, interests and ideas and can occur through unconscious influences such as body language and linguistic emphases. Children will remember an enthusiastic teacher, and this enthusiasm will influence the children's interest in the subject. Negative attitudes to science may adversely affect both the children's interest and subsequent development. It is therefore important that all practitioners have positive attitudes to science and science teaching in order to teach effectively and develop positive attitudes in the children they teach. Practitioners' attitudes to science have developed in a similar way to those of the children they teach and result from a complex of experiences gathered throughout their lives, each with the potential to affect their attitudes in a different way. Very young children could be experiencing gravity through dropping objects out of their pram. This may be a very stimulating experience for them and end up being a game played with adults. As they grow older they will have a variety of formal and informal science experiences which develop this initial idea. They may make paper aeroplanes or explore the forces in the water trough or bath. They may watch television programmes or read textbooks about gravity and air resistance. Some of these experiences may be positive and some negative and all provide information about science. Together they provide an overall view about science which will result in an attitude to science.

I have been aware of the effect of negative attitudes to science from my own school experiences and from my earliest days of primary teaching. My own background was one of varied science experiences. As a primary child I was part of the Nuffield Primary Science Project (1964–6) and have memories of exciting science experiences. I can vividly remember, as an eleven-year-old, being very excited about the prospect of learning science in the secondary school, but by the end of (what is now) Year 7 I hated science. This affected my subsequent achievement in these areas until, at a later date, I discovered the positive side of science through teaching. My own research (Johnston *et al.*, 1998; Johnston and Ahtee, 2005) is confirming the importance of positive attitudes to science for scientific development and the effect attitudes can have on the development of concepts and skills in science at every stage of development from the early years through to initial and continuing professional development. Since I have worked in initial and continuing teacher education, I have become very concerned about the attitudes to science prevailing within the teaching community. As a primary school teacher I spent considerable time alleviating fears about science among my colleagues. At initial teacher training level, I have realized that many future teachers are fearful and concerned about science and teaching science in the primary classroom (Johnston and Ahtee, 2005). Comments from primary initial teacher training students about the nature of science have included:

> If it's science we are expected to . . .
> There's got to be a right answer.
> I hate science, it's boring.
> I can't do science, it's really hard.

These attitudes to science will be difficult to hide in the classroom and will inevitably have an effect on the children we teach. Once, when working within the environment, initial teaching students were asked to observe minibeasts and to carry out an investigation on the basis of their initial observations and explorations. One group decided to investigate which surfaces snails preferred. They designed an investigation which looked at the snails at regular intervals and noted where they were. After some time I asked them what they had discovered, and the reply was that the data collected had not been conclusive. I then asked them what surface they felt the snails preferred and they replied without hesitation 'the damp one . . . they went in there more often'. This example illustrated the students' views on the nature of science. It was about hard quantitative data, the only valid evidence being that collected at regular time intervals, with anything else being rejected as 'unscientific'. More recently research with student teachers

(Ahtee and Johnston, 2005; Johnston and Ahtee, 2005) has demonstrated the need for quality teacher education, firstly forming positive attitudes, then focusing on subject knowledge and pedagogical content knowledge in a meaningful way.

Expectations

Children's expectations of science are the result of science experiences inside and outside school. They come to expect science to mean doing or watching an investigation and drawing a picture or writing about it. Jarvis (1994) found that young children, when asked to draw pictures of scientists, often drew pictures of themselves or their teachers in school involved in a scientific activity. For these children science was something that happened in school. Those who drew the teacher appeared to view science as passive, with the teacher doing science for them, while those who drew themselves expected to be active participatory scientists. Some children also drew artists, and Jarvis (1994) felt that this was a result of the children being asked to draw a picture about their science activity. We do a science activity and then draw a picture. Therefore children believe science equals art.

Media

The media can have an important effect in the development of both scientific ideas and attitudes. Unfortunately, not all media images of science and scientists are positive. Children will recognize the mad scientist in media representations − the white-coated boffin described earlier in this chapter. The picture in Figure 4.5 was drawn in response to my son's description of a scientist. As a Year 3 child he asked me 'Are you a real scientist, mummy?' He then went on to explain that he considered a 'real scientist' to 'have something to do with chemicals and things' (Johnston, 1992). He had been influenced by his limited experiences, which included television portrayals of scientists. When he saw the picture in Figure 4.5 he said 'That's a scientist'. I was dismayed by this narrow view of science and scientists even in such a young child and I was concerned with the number of children who acquire this view from the media and then have few other influences that challenge it. As children develop, the media view of science may, together with school experiences, confirm a view of science that is negative in nature. These views can be seen in young children through their descriptions and pictures of scientists, who when there were a large number of reality vet programmes on television drew pictures of scientists in laboratory coats with animals and said that 'scientists work with cats and dogs'. Television adverts and science fiction films often depict scientists in a stereotypical way and this sends less positive messages to children. We obviously cannot influence the way science and scientists are depicted in the media, but we can be aware of the effects on children's images of science.

There are a large number of science-focused programmes on television, many of which interest young children and influence their subsequent attitudes, especially if they can follow these up themselves by observing or experiencing scientific phenomena in their own environments. However, some of these programmes tackle very difficult and abstract ideas in a very simplistic or sensational way and this can adversely affect children's ideas and attitudes, especially if the ideas cannot be experienced or understood in the child's world or if the programme confuses rather than motivates the children.

Figure 4.5   A scientist?

Gender

Gender can affect attitudes through both genetic and social influences. There are many differences observed between boys and girls from a very young age (Berk, 2003) and these include attitudes or have a knock-on effect on attitudes (see Table 4.1). Some of the gender differences in attitudes could have genetic origins (for example timidity, independence and assertiveness), while others are likely to be the result of social interaction (achievement motivation), or even be genetic tendencies reinforced by nurture (dominance and submissiveness). Certainly, the commonly held view in 30 different countries around the world is that boys have more instrumental traits (reflecting competence, assertiveness and competitiveness) and girls have more expressive traits (reflecting care, sensitivity and consideration of others) and this will affect behaviour towards boys and girls and their subsequence behaviour (Williams and Best, 1990; Ross and Browne, 1993). In schools, gender differences have been found (Dean, 2001) in development, achievement and teacher attention and single-sexed teaching to have positive advantages, especially for boys who underachieve (Sukhnandan *et al.*, 2000). From an early age girls can be discouraged from enjoying and achieving success in science by negative attitudes to science, both held by them and by those around them, although girls do tend to take education in general more seriously than boys (Tinklin, 2003). Gender differences in attitudes have been found at all levels of development (Smail, 1984; Catsambis, 1995). The development of attitudes to science is thought to occur early (Smail, 1984). Toys given to children send gender messages to them, and a child who uses construction toys and an electricity kit is likely to be confident and more able in science in the same way that one who plays with a doll is likely to be a more confident parent. Pre-school experience, together with role models, peer attitude, the media and a complex of other influences, means that girls often have a poor attitude and poor achievement in science subjects. Sometimes girls are discouraged by parents and teachers from taking science subjects. It is hardly surprising that this trend is reflected in the percentage of girls studying balanced science (biology, chemistry and physics) (Wallace, 1994) at advanced (Head, 1996) and undergraduate level (Gold, 1990).

The effect of gender attitude differences can be seen in young children. For example, Year 2 boys are more likely to find the correct solution to the climbing man problem described in Chapter 3. Girls are more likely to observe phenomena closely, especially in the environment, and to draw or write what they observe. Girls too, are more likely to play and explore co-operatively and accept the views of others, while boys are more likely to generate creative ideas and be more forceful in trying out their ideas.

Table 4.1 Gender differences and the effect on early scientific development

Characteristic	Gender differences	Effect on early scientific development
Verbal abilities	Girls develop language and reading abilities at an earlier age than boys.	Girls are more likely to develop scientific language earlier and perform better in explorations and assessments that are language dependent.
Spatial abilities	Boys display better spatial abilities throughout life.	Boys may be able to mental model more abstract scientific ideas.
Mathematical abilities	From adolescence onwards boys out-perform girls in mathematical reasoning.	
School achievement	Girls get better grades in all academic subjects at primary level and generally better at secondary level.	Girls will enter Key Stages 1 and 2 with higher assessment levels.
Emotional sensitivity	Girls are more sensitive to emotional signals and score higher in measures of empathy and sympathy.	Girls tend to relate to more biological sciences.
Achievement motivation	Girls perceive themselves as more competent at reading, writing art, etc. and therefore are more motivated. Boys perceive themselves as more competent (and are more motivated) in mathematics, sports and mechanical subjects.	Boys are often more motivated in science explorations especially if more physics and chemistry orientated.
Fear, anxiety	Girls are more timid than boys, while boys are more likely to be risk takers.	Boys are more likely to have creative ideas in science.
Compliance and dependency	Girls are more compliant and will allow themselves to be directed by adults and peers. They also seek more help than boys.	Girls are likely to work more co-operatively in group situations and allow others to lead. Boys are more likely to assume leadership in science explorations.

Characteristic	Gender differences	Effect on early scientific development
Activity level	Boys are more active than girls.	Boys appear to enjoy more practical, kinaesthetic explorations.
Aggression	Boys are more openly aggressive than girls.	They are likely to find social explorations more difficult.
Disabilities	Boys are more likely to have physical disabilities, mental retardation and developmental delay.	Boys are more likely to need individual support in science explorations.

Culture and religious beliefs

Cultural values can have a very large influence on early attitude development (see Berk, 2003), especially where the values of home and the child's identity conflict with the values of the educational setting (Siraj-Blatchford, 2000). This alone will slow development, but will be greater where the scientific values of home also conflict with the values traditionally viewed to be held by scientists. Science learning does not simply consist of acceptance of imparted ideas, especially when those ideas conflict with beliefs. Children may find ideas expressed within school controversial (Reiss, 1993; Aikenhead, 2000) and they may even conflict with their beliefs, causing some conflict and alienation. Care has been taken that the Foundation Stage Curriculum (QCA, 2000) does not conflict with home culture and there is plenty of guidance for practitioners (see for example, Moyles and Adams, 2001) and to develop attitudes such as respect and tolerance. The science content embodied within the National Curriculum (DfEE, 1999) contains much that conflicts with the values held by some people within our society. However, analysis of the science content of the National Curriculum not only identifies the conflicts but, together with consideration of the questions raised earlier in this chapter, can help individuals to decide on their view of the nature of science. Sc 1 (Scientific Enquiry) deals in part with the nature of science, which can be perceived in a variety of ways and will be affected by individual values. Is science about knowledge, facts and high intelligence? Is it creative and exploratory or repetitive and predictable? If children's views of the nature of science and scientists are limited, then it seems likely that their development as scientists will be affected. Sc 2 (Life Processes and Living Things) involves consideration of a number of ethical issues. The subject of evolution (creation versus natural selection) can cause conflict, as can the area of reproduction and sex education and environmental issues such as recycling, which also form part of citizenship at later levels (DfEE, 1999). Consideration of these issues may touch upon sensitive areas of personal, political and economic concern (Chapman, 1991) and will help children to become citizens of the future and to develop attitudes such as respect for others, tolerance of ideas and beliefs and sensitivity.

Sc 3 (Materials and their Properties) involves work with materials and food technology and could expose conflicts regarding food beliefs. I once made the mistake of looking at the science involved in the baking process during Ramadan when a Muslim girl was fasting. Other food preferences need to be taken into consideration, as well as food allergies. Vegetarians would not welcome making bread with animal fat and sweets may put diabetics at risk. Again careful interaction can support the development of both social and reflective/cognitive attitudes.

The Earth and Beyond in Sc 4 (Physical Processes) is not identified as a requirement for Key Stage 1 children (DfEE, 1999), although often used as a focus for play and development. It poses additional problems concerned with scientific views of the birth of the universe, as compared to some religious teaching. Even as teachers of young children we cannot ignore these issues if they arise in the classroom, if for no other reason than that children will not stop asking profound questions about their origin even if the National Curriculum does not encourage it.

These areas of potential conflict make it necessary for all primary teachers to be aware of the need for sensitivity in teaching many aspects of science. Care needs to be taken to ensure that we do not indoctrinate children with our own cultural opinions, but provide a balanced view. The same areas of science can also provide opportunities to promote cultural similarities and celebrate and respect differences, and this should also be remembered. For example, within Sc 1 learning about scientists and the stories of science will help children to realize the differing views held by scientists and the differing lives of scientists. Children find the stories fascinating and are appalled to realize society's unjust treatment of some scientists. Antonouris (1991) and Reiss (1993) describe the life of Charles Drew, the black scientist who developed the blood bank and was then denied blood after a car crash. The stories of Marie Curie, Albert Einstein and many other famous scientists throughout the centuries can be retold easily to children of all ages, and make science and scientists more attainable and understandable for the average child. Children are more likely to remember the science if they can relate to the scientist. Learning about science is as important as learning science, and children need to have access to stories about scientific discoveries, theories and people. This will help them to realize that scientists are normal human beings, that science is relevant to their lives (Reiss, 1993), that science is not something that is only carried out by scientists in laboratories. I often tell the story of Darwin's voyage on the Beagle (Johnston and Gray, 1999) to early-years children and we observe and sort a collection of pictures of animals and animal bones (see Chapter 1). Even very young children can engage with Darwin's story and can begin to develop their own ideas about the similarities between animals, which can be grouped together in families. In doing this, children can develop reflective and social attitudes, such as objectivity, tolerance and respect. When sorting pictures of animals with Reception children, Amy grouped all the animals with big teeth together (cat, lion, crocodile, bear), Sean collected the animals with wings (birds, including ostrich, kingfisher, blackbird and a bat), and Patrick the ones that looked like horses (donkey, horse, zebra). Older children are likely to be able to sort by more than one criterion and can make additional groupings, or assign one animal to more than one group, such as those that live in water (fish, whale, dolphin, crocodile), those with fur (cat, dog, bear, lion) or those that eat vegetation (cow, sheep, horse, donkey, zebra) and those that eat meat (cat, dog, lion, crocodile).

In Sc 2 children can explore the similarities and differences between themselves (see also Siraj-Blatchford, 2000). Shoe size, head size, height, food preferences and interests can be compared with beliefs and celebrations. There are some good activities that illustrate both similarities and differences. Focus on observable physical differences and similarities can lead to greater tolerance about differences, but care needs to be taken to ensure that differences are not ridiculed and that children are not made to feel inadequate. I have set up the home corner to include family photographs, a photograph album and a family tree (Johnston and Herridge, 2004, see also chapter 3). It is good to use cartoon or stylized pictures, including family members from different cultures and I try to include a mixture of ages and gender, so there are pictures of grandparents, parents, aunts, uncles, cousins, sisters, brothers, etc. The children sort the pictures and put them into the album and on to the family tree. Discussion has focused on different family members and different types of families from nuclear, extended, single-parent, large, small and also the family resemblances, the ages of family members and the human life cycle. All this can be done while the children are playing in the home corner. I asked Sameena to show me her family album and she talked about the fictional pictures, describing the extended family who lived with her and all her cousins who lived in 'a long way away'. She told me that she looked like her aunty and her sister looked like her mother. While she was doing this, Daisy listened attentively and chipped in to say 'I have my mommy's eyes' and that her grandmother lived in another house nearby.

In Sc 3 (Materials and their Properties), the play in the home area can be extended to look at food preferences and food celebrations, supporting the development of cultural awareness. Again care needs to be taken to ensure that differences are treated sensitively and that beliefs are not ridiculed, but again sensitive interaction can support the development of social and reflective/cognitive attitudes (see Figure 4.2). Children can be encouraged to prepare for different cultural and religious festivals and prepare the home corner, food and clothes for the occasion. In making the celebratory food, the children can look at the materials and how they change when mixed, heated or cooled and what they taste like. They can also consider the similarities and differences between the celebratory food being prepared and the food from their own culture (see Moyles and Adams, 2001).

A conflict of beliefs also exists within Sc 4 (Physical Processes), where study of the Earth and Beyond may expose different cultural and religious ideas. While this is an area not necessarily looked at closely in the early years, many children like to explore space, the moon, sun and the planets and settings often set up space play for children, which may expose these ideas. However, sensitive handling can promote not only cultural awareness but also tolerance and acceptance.

Friends

It would be foolish to believe that children were not influenced by their peers. If friends have negative attitudes to science then this may influence children's attitudes, especially as they are forming. Peer-group pressures can influence children's development in the classroom in a number of ways. If the classroom atmosphere is not conducive to asking questions then children are less likely to raise questions. If the class considers science to be boring and useless or only for the boys, then children may not challenge this view because they would not wish to appear different from their peers. They may believe that this view is expected of them and conform in this way. Encouraging children to play and explore co-operatively can support the development of social attitudes such as, co-operation, collaboration, tolerance, independence and responsibility. Explorations of a group of children can help to develop these attitudes alongside understandings and skills. For example, comparisons of individual passports (described in Chapter 3 and Figure 3.3) can help children to recognize that we have much in common as well as individual differences (see also Siraj-Blatchford, 2000). The work can be extended to consider the range of hair and skin colours (I use paint colour charts to see the range of colours) and answer questions, such as,

- Are older children taller?
- Can the biggest children jump the highest?
- Do boys have bigger hands?
- Can girls skip for longer?

Ability/disability

Children's abilities and disabilities will affect their attitudes. If a child is successful and achieves well in their explorations they will be motivated to continue to explore and develop skills, understandings and other attitudes. If a child is unable to participate fully or explore because of disability of any kind, they will become frustrated and this will adversely affect their motivation and subsequent development. Additionally, if a child finds the level of engagement is not sufficient for them and the

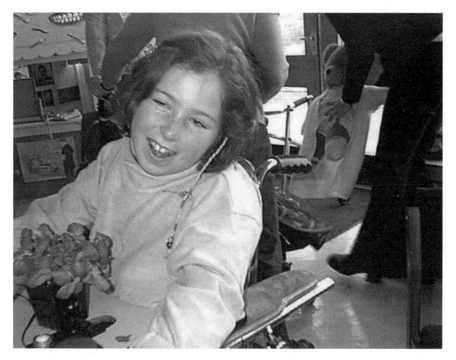

Picture 4.2   *A physically disabled child exploring in the smell of herbs*

exploration is pitched at too simplistic a level, they may become bored and demotivated. The importance of catering for individual needs is well recognized (QCA, 2000; Wolfendale *et al.*, 2000; DfES, 2003) and catering for the range of needs in any setting is an increasing problem. The issues of differentiating explorations and supporting play and exploration are discussed more fully in Chapter 6. Children with physical disabilities need activities differentiated to accommodate their disability and without assuming that physical disability means cognitive disability. While working with children in a school for children with severe physical disabilities, students adapted science activities, although some found the challenge of preparing and adapting activities for individual needs difficult. On the theme of illusions, one student prepared optical illusions to make, although some children were unable to manage fine motor activities and some had visual impairments. This does not mean that the children could not look at illusions but the focus needed to be on the different and sometimes misleading feel of textiles on the skin, the different way warm water feels if our hands are hot or cold, or the way different smells or colours can deceive our taste buds (we expect lemon tastes to be yellow and fruity smells to be fruity tasting).

A multifaceted approach to developing positive attitudes to science

Developing attitudes to science needs to take into account the different influences on that development; to engage in a multifaceted approach to the development of attitudes. It needs to consider the development of attitudes in teachers, parents and children. Teacher training, both initial training and inservice, needs to focus on what positive attitudes to science are, whether we have positive attitudes and how they can be developed in the children we teach. School curricular developments should help to improve children's attitudes through good teaching, creative, exploratory activities, sensitivity to the values and opinions of others, school visits and special events such as science and technology weeks and inter-school or community collaborations. The development of positive parental attitudes can involve greater participation in school science. They can include home–school science liaison and special school events to focus on science in the curriculum or the nature of science, such as science fairs and industry links (Woolnough, 1994).

Family science activities can promote positive home–school liaison and good scientific attitudes in both children and the wider community. They can also develop a better understanding of science education, its purposes, constraints and even an understanding of the nature of science. For example, one group of parents was observed responding to the

Picture 4.3   *Developing attitudes through play and interaction*

question, 'How can you make light shine round a corner?', by using mirrors that had been joined together to put into a kaleidoscope. It appeared that they felt that the problem must involve some complex scientific equipment. Another parent observing this interaction commented 'Did you ever do that at school? Use a mirror to shine a light in someone's face?' The response was 'Oh yes, but I didn't think that was science.'

Success in developing positive attitudes in science and to science depends on all parties concerned in the process – parents, teachers, children and society. We all need to play our part and this has become easier as the introduction of the Foundation Stage curriculum (QCA, 2000) and the primary strategy (DfES, 2003) has renewed interest in and stressed the importance of affective development and a multifaceted approach, through principles which emphasize social, emotional and cultural development.

Summary

- Positive attitudes are essential to enable children to develop scientifically.
- Scientific attitudes can be categorized into motivating attitudes, social attitudes, practical attitudes and reflective attitudes.
- Attitudes to science are the result of a complex of influences on children's lives. Work to develop attitudes to science should adopt a multifaceted approach which addresses these influences.

5

Creative early experiences

We should develop a creative teaching approach which challenges stereotyped views of science and, most importantly, clearly develops knowledge alongside attitudes and skills. The importance of creativity in teaching is now widely acknowledged (see DfES, 2003; QCA, 2003a; Feasey, 2003; ASE, 2004). It is more important than ever to provide creative, stimulating activities in order to motivate children and assist the development of their scientific concepts, skills and attitudes. This can be difficult because children are often very demanding in their need for motivation.

Motivating children is possibly one of the biggest challenges teachers have to meet, and it does seem to be more and more important and more and more difficult to achieve. One of the reasons why stimulating science activities are necessary and difficult to provide is concerned with the incredible competition we face as teachers. Sophisticated television programmes and interactive books provide stimuli of a very high calibre. Interactive science centres are springing up all over Britain with resources that schools cannot possibly match. Computers, videos and compact discs are available in many homes, and children have access to a wide range of software, which they understand and which provides opportunities for them to experience the impossible – a trip through the solar system or a journey through a rainforest, for example. Shops sell a wide range of children's toys and science kits which cover all areas of science and enable children, for example, to experience electricity by making their own solar-powered toys, potato clocks or radios or to experience forces or energy through a variety of home-made toys. Changes in society with regard to employment, finances and household aids mean that children often have a larger number of adults and peers to interact with. As a result, children are immersed in science from an early age and by the time they arrive in school they will have had a large number of informal and formal science experiences and will have built up a large amount of tacit knowledge, as described in Chapter 1.

Today's children have plenty of resources, both human, paper, electronic and otherwise, to stimulate their senses. They have become dependent on sensory stimulation and are very critical of activities that are not motivating and exciting. Educational and organizational considerations provide a possible reason why stimulating science activities are difficult to deliver in the classroom context. It is a hard task to provide original, motivating ideas which enthuse the children, are manageable in the school context and have a valid and easily accessed teaching and learning point. The task is not made easier by curricular changes (DfEE, 1999; QCA, 2000), national strategies in literacy (DfEE, 1998), numeracy (DfEE, 1999a) and the primary strategy (DfES, 2003) which have changed the structure of early education and sent anomalous messages about the nature of teaching and learning. The introduction of the national literacy and numeracy strategies, together with the QCA schemes of work in science (QCA, 2000a) turned the role of the practitioner into more of a technician than a creative motivator, developer and teacher. Some early-years settings began to have a more formal appearance and for many play and exploration were replaced by demonstration with the child-centred education of the past becoming a curriculum and knowledge-based focus. The Foundation Curriculum (QCA, 2000) redressed the balance and emphasized the importance of creative exploration for effective early development. The primary strategy (DfES, 2003: 29), identified the principles of effective primary education, including:

- making learning vivid and real, by developing understanding through enquiry, creativity, e-learning and group problem-solving;
- making learning an enjoyable and challenging experience, by stimulating learning through matching teaching to learning styles and preferences;
- enriching the learning experience, by developing learning skills across the curriculum.

The strategy stresses the importance of literacy and numeracy, but emphasizes the importance of teachers 'adapting and shaping them to their own pupil needs' (DfES, 2003: 27). For many practitioners in the Foundation Stage and particularly at Key Stage 1, this poses a dilemma: how to incorporate the features of effective creative practice, but maintain the rigour and focus on key objectives for development and learning.

Scientific concepts, knowledge and skills are fairly unchanging and so it might seem that original science activities are almost impossible to deliver. We need to remember that while most science activities are 'old favourites' of ours, for many children they will be new experiences, and that creativity and originality apply not only to the activities we prepare for children to experience but also to our teaching. We can be original and creative in the provision of science activities, especially when we become confident ourselves in scientific understanding. Every teacher has the potential for originality and creativity, but too often we are constrained by our lack of science knowledge and a poor understanding of what science is and are unable to use our creativity in the classroom context. Primary teachers do not, generally, have a strong science background (Ginn and Watters, 1995; Harlen and Holroyd, 1997) and there is increasing concern about the scientific knowledge possessed by students training in primary education (Trumper, 2003) and pedagogical content knowledge (Johnston & Ahtee, 2005). We are also pressurized by the demands of an ever increasing curriculum, and with its accompanying assessment procedures and its focus on targets, it is often difficult to be original and creative. Lesson plans that can be downloaded from the internet can appear to ease workload, but they need careful adaptation to make them creative and match the needs of specific children. As a result, the planning and organization of creative science activities can appear daunting. If we are not successful in planning and organizational terms, we may suffer the effects of indiscipline and disorganization to the effect that learning objectives will not be achieved, the children will be out of our control and the resulting chaos will be a threat to our sanity.

This is not a pretty scenario and one that we would want to avoid. However, the result of not providing creative activities can be disastrous in other ways, too. We may be perpetuating the traditional view of science and science education as a discipline that is boring, factual and difficult. We may have a peaceful classroom, (although in my experience bored children are disruptive ones), but if we do not motivate the children they will view science in a negative way and this may influence them in their future learning. There have been concerns that enthusiasm for science is dwindling and that young people are not taking up science options at A-level and university (see Chapter 4). If children are not motivated then it is sensible to conclude that learning will be impaired. The importance of motivation is recognized by many (e.g. Bricheno *et al*, 2000; DfES, 2003) and Harlen (2000) looks further at the part played by intrinsic motivation in the learning process, arguing that if a learner is not motivated to learn then the learning potential is immaterial.

Originality and creativity

What do we mean by 'originality' and 'creativity' in the provision of scientific activities? Originality and creativity are difficult to define because they have been taken to be synonymous (Childs, 1986) and because they are often used to mean different things in different contexts, for example art, technology and science. However, Prentice (2000) identifies that creativity is not exclusive to the arts and de Bono (1992) has extended the definition of creativity to thinking and problem-solving. The dictionary definition of originality is concerned with the initiation of new ideas, design or style, while creativity is concerned with bringing into being or making something new. It can be argued that originality is the essence of creativity. There are disputes among psychologists as to whether creativity and originality are characteristics of the highly intelligent (Munn, 1966; Childs, 1986) or a potential in all of us which needs encouragement and motivation to flourish (Medawar, 1969). Duffy (1998) considers making connections as an important aspect of creativity and this is an important aspect of creative teaching as practitioners need to make the connections between aspects of learning across the curriculum (DfES, 2003). Practitioners with little ability to provide original and creative science activities would have only a basic familiarity with the subject skills, concepts and knowledge and would have few ideas of their own. They would be dependent on others for ideas about what to develop and how to develop it. As practitioners' subject competence increases and they become more knowledgeable about the skills, concepts and knowledge involved, they are able to extend or adapt ideas which are given to them. They may not be able to initiate original and creative activities but they will be able constructively to change them to meet children's needs. The most original and creative providers of primary science activities would have an insight into the subject and an understanding of how to teach it. They would be able to make their own decisions about teaching styles and learning experiences, producing novel ideas for achieving objectives and as a result the children's learning will be enhanced (QCA, 2000). They would also be enthusiastic about the subject and the teaching of that subject and would balance the needs of the curriculum with those of the individual's creative development, balancing creativity and knowledge (Boden, 2001). Fraser and Tobin (1993) have identified features of exemplary Australian primary and secondary science teachers. These teachers were identified by asking other teachers, advisory staff and educators. Those nominated managed their classrooms effectively, used teaching strategies that focused on the children's understanding, provided learning environments that suited the children's learning preferences, had a strong content knowledge and encouraged children's involvement in classroom discussions and activities.

Encouraging and motivating children's scientific thinking

Providing different ways to package science ideas can help motivate children and encourage them to think about the science involved. We do not always have to provide 'hands-on' activities; we can promote discussion and thought in other ways. Occasionally, I don a pointed hat and, waving my magic wand, tell a class of primary children that I am going to show them some magic. I then conduct a series of 'magic tricks', all within a scientific theme. Once, focusing on forces, with the help of my magic wand I turned a cup of water, with a piece of card on top, upside down without spilling a drop; made a hard-boiled egg go into a bottle without touching or breaking it, made a small Lego diver drop to the bottom of a bottle of water and made a model person climb up some string. The children took great delight in explaining why I was not the world's greatest magician and why the 'tricks' worked. One child even said 'It isn't magic, it's science.' This was the most important part of this activity and provided the opportunity for the children to express their own ideas and actually challenged some of them. It was extremely important to explore the science behind each activity.

For the paper and cup 'trick' you fill a cup as full as possible with water and place a small piece of card over the top. When carefully turned over (Figure 5.1) the card remains over the opening and the water inside the cup. This is because the forces acting on the cup and card are balanced. If the downward forces are greater the water spills out of the cup. It is therefore advisable to do this over a sink or bowl. Some children hypothesized that the cup was 'sticky' and that I had 'cheated'. Some children were able to identify the forces involved: 'It's the air pushing it up.' They did not really focus on all the forces involved, but as an activity to introduce forces it was motivating and challenging. I did advise them to try it out over a sink if they wanted to 'have a go' at home, and while I gather there were some wet tables, parents were generally pleased with the interest their children showed. I suppose this approach to science must have motivated the children because, years later, I would occasionally get young adults saying 'Do you remember when ...?' Having fun was very important and motivating, but the most important

Figure 5.1   The paper and cup activity

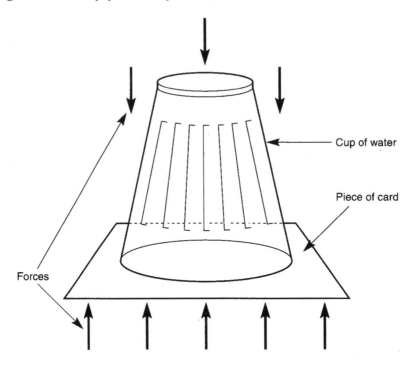

Cup of water

Piece of card

Forces

part of the activity involved the explaining. It was essential to allow the children time to discuss their ideas; to draw conclusions about the science inherent in the activities; to interpret their findings and forward their conceptual development.

For the egg and bottle 'trick' you use a hard-boiled egg (shell removed) and a glass bottle with a wide neck. Check that the egg sits snugly in the opening of the bottle (Figure 5.2). Place a lighted match or taper in the bottle and put the egg back over the opening. The match or taper will go out and the egg will 'plop' into the bottle. As with the paper and cup activity, the underlying concept is forces. The egg should be only slightly bigger than the opening of the bottle, and it is forced into the bottle because the downward forces acting on the egg are greater than the upward forces. The balance of the forces changes when the air inside the bottle is heated and expands, escaping around the egg. As the air cools down the air pressure on the outside of the bottle is greater than on the inside and the egg is forced through the opening. The egg can be removed by increasing the pressure inside the bottle by blowing into the up-ended bottle, but only try this if the egg has gone into the bottle

Figure 5.2 The egg and bottle activity

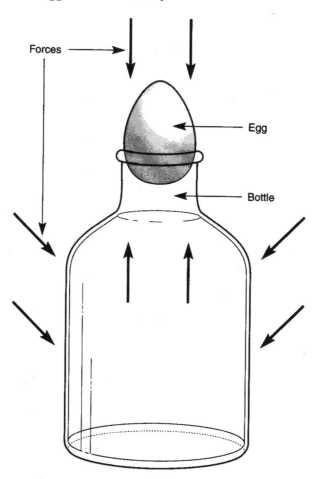

whole and intact. The children were fascinated by this display of 'magic' but the magician's guise did not fool them and they were convinced that there was a logical explanation and began to look for it. I attempted to focus their discussions so that the forces involved were considered. Sometimes, especially with older children, some misconceptions were highlighted; mainly the idea that some of the gas, usually the oxygen, had been used up, creating an unequal force. It was important that I did not encourage this misconception, and further follow-up work was needed to challenge these ideas. Children did not need to leave the activity with full understanding of the science involved, but it was important that they did not leave with misconceptions. Thought-provoking activities which make children think about the relevant concept are more likely to lead to later understanding.

The Lego diver activity is a version of the Cartesian diver. The Lego diver would have an upside-down test-tube attached to its back with a rubber band. The diver was then carefully inserted into a wide-necked plastic bottle full of water so that it floated, just under the water, at the top of the bottle (Figure 5.3). When the bottle was squeezed the diver would sink to the bottom of the bottle and when the pressure was released, would float back up to the top. After the initial excitement, the children would explore the diver for themselves; this would lead to some good observations being made and some simple hypotheses being developed.

Look! it works when I squeeze it.
The bubble gets smaller.

When asked why they thought the air bubble inside the test-tube got smaller they responded:

The water pushes it up.
You are squashing the water inside.
It hasn't got much room when you squeeze it.

This could then be related to their experiences in the water trough and to ideas they had about floating and sinking. Usually this consisted of the hypothesis that heavy things would sink and light things would float. Further investigation in the water trough could challenge this idea. This might include changing the shape of a ball of dough or plasticine so that it would alternately sink or float in the water, or taking a piece of aluminium foil and making it sink by squashing it up tightly.

For the climber activity (see also Chapter 3), the climber needs to be made out of sturdy card and the shape should not be flimsy or have thin arms. Small pieces of drinking straws can be taped in place on the arms of the climber and string or strong cotton threaded through the straws. The top ends of the string should be fastened to a piece of card and the bottom ends weighted with plasticine (Figure 5.4). The children I worked with were able to make the climber climb up the string by holding the top of the model and rotating their wrist slightly. They were keen to make one for themselves, and in order to do so successfully they needed to explore the forces involved. There were two critical factors in making a successful climber, the first being the angle of the straws and the second being the mass of the plasticine. The straws need to be angled in for the person to climb up the string. If the straws were angled outwards the climber would not climb but would descend the string. This surprised the children, and they were then encouraged to examine why this happens.

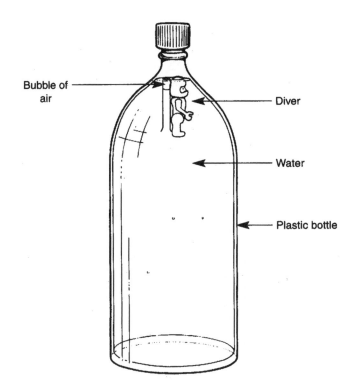

Figure 5.3 The Lego diver activity

Closer examination allowed them to see that the straw should be angled in such a way that with a movement of the wrist it becomes vertical and allows the string to drop through. The mass of the plasticine should be enough to allow the string to drop through the straw when the straw is vertical, but not so great as to affect the strength of the card or force the string through the straw. I have used this activity when exploring forces through a topic on Victorians. We explored a range of Victorian toys and looked at the forces involved and then made our 'climbers' in the shape of little chimney-sweep boys who climbed up the chimney.

Once with Year 1 and 2 children we made Father Christmas climbers who climbed up to the roof. On another occasion Year 2 children designed their own 'climbers' and the resulting designs included an underwater diver who went down from a boat, a spiderman who climbed up to his web and a monkey who climbed up a tree. These excellent activities have also provided meaningful and creative links with both technology and history. In one Year 1 class we were exploring the forces

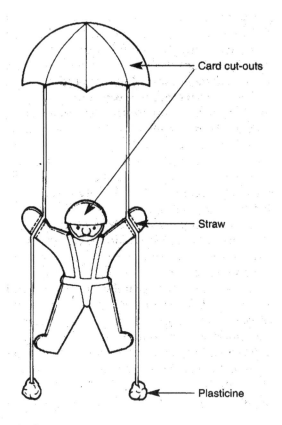

Figure 5.4   The climber activity

involved in a collection of moving toys and made climbing men. At the time, the English football team were playing in the World Cup and some of the children chose to make David Beckham jumping for joy because he had scored a goal. One boy (see Picture 5.1) proudly showed me his David Beckham, complete with Mohican haircut, made by cutting out an extra piece of paper and drawing hair on it and sticking it on his head!

With each of these activities it has been most important to explore the science that underpins them. Without this underpinning the activity becomes educationally meaningless despite being creative and stimulating.

Visiting schools in England and other parts of the world has shown me the importance of stimulating, creative science activities which enthuse children and encourage them to investigate scientific phenomena in greater depth. I have witnessed some stimulating environments created in the classroom, bringing artefacts in, and taking children outside to

Picture 5.1   *Year 1 child with David Beckham climbing man*

provide more visually interactive displays to capture attention. I applaud any motivating force that encourages the children in their explorations, but my main concern is that they should not just be stimulating contexts, but that scientific development should be enhanced through these activities.

There are many science activities that appear creative and stimulating and the children appear absorbed, motivated and entertained even though the actual scientific development occurring is small. Sometimes confusion occurs because a creative simulation or analogy is used. I have seen a potentially interesting science activity on the theme of earth sciences which looked at volcanoes. A simulation of a volcano was achieved using jam tarts which when cooked behaved in a similar way to an erupting volcano. Those involved were having great fun and it was possible that the analogy between jam tarts and volcanoes was made explicit in some minds, but I was not convinced. In most minds the actual knowledge about volcanic eruptions and their geological links was not made explicit and the activity was 'fun' rather than developing scientific knowledge. Rather than using simulations, it is better to support the children in developing their own models to express scientific phenomena (see Chapter 3).

We need to take care that activities we use in school, while remaining creative and motivating and identifying the magic of science, illustrate a positive view of science and have a specific learning intention which remains at the centre of all teaching and which is at the forefront of any assessment. We need to provide positive science experiences for our children, but there does need to be an educational justification for 'entertaining science'. I would advocate creative science teaching, believing strongly that learning is enhanced by the provision of activities that are 'interesting and thought-provoking, and which can harness the child's natural curiosity and questioning' (Raper and Stringer, 1987: 20), but creative activities should emphasize the importance of a clearly identified learning intention. It is the ability to determine the learning intention and to plan for this which characterizes teaching as opposed to entertainment or childcare. This theme is further developed in Chapter 6, but it is important that we stress here, in looking at creativity in science activities, the importance of learning through enjoyment and that enjoyable activities are not always synonymous with learning.

Creative science, information and communication technology and the media

Children are often at ease with and stimulated by information and communication technology (ICT), while many teachers do not find it at all friendly. ICT has been found (Bowell *et al.*, 1994; Cook and Finlayson, 1999; Ager, 2000) to motivate and stimulate and result in many positive learning outcomes, such as an increase in both the quality and quantity of written work, pupil effort, motivation and confidence. Children in primary schools today are growing up in a world of high technology and they do not seem to find the pace of change as confusing as adults do. ICT can provide a stimulating way to develop scientific skills as well as scientific concepts and knowledge and, as the DfES (2003: 29) say, we should 'make learning vivid and real' by developing 'understanding through enquiry, creativity, e-learning and group problem solving'. The role of ICT in creative teaching and learning has not been fully explored, but

Craft (2002) does feel that it has the capacity to enhance children's individual creativity.

There is a wide range of computer software and interactive videos which allow children to access scientific information and view scientific phenomena. Encyclopaedia CD-ROMs use and contain huge amounts of data, some in picture form appropriate for young children. ICT can also encourage observational skills, provide help with children's planning and recording, assist in their investigations and provide opportunities for the interpretation of data. In this way ICT can help to develop scientific skills as well as scientific knowledge in a motivating context.

Observational skills and the ability to raise questions can be developed through the use of a computer microscope (as described in Chapter 1) or a good computer database program. Databases can help children to observe closely, to raise questions and to group according to observable features. There are two types of database which can achieve this development: hierarchical or branch databases, which compare one object to another by looking at a number of different attributes; and relational databases, which look at the relationship between objects, enabling children to group them according to observable features and begin to make and use simple keys. Some of these are closed or ready-made databases, which can be used to observe a specific group of things or which already contain data, while others are open and can be used to observe and classify a range of objects. They range from simple databases which are very suitable for children in the early years to complex databases which are more difficult to operate and contain a wide range of data.

Children do need to have experience of databases before using computer databases. It can be fun to map out a branch database on paper and then transfer it to a computer database. Children can start with a collection of fruit or moving toys (see Chapter 2) and begin to look for similarities and differences. They can begin to map out a simple branch database on paper or on the floor by asking questions, the answers to which will differentiate the objects. As in Chapter 2, a collection of moving toys can be differentiated by asking questions such as,

- Is it magnetic?
- Does it spin?
- Does it use electricity?

These questions can be raised by the children, written on cards by the teacher and placed by sorting hoops. The toys can then be sorted into sorting hoops (see Picture 5.2).

Given a collection of fruit, for example, a banana, apple, pear, strawberry, kiwi fruit, avocado, star fruit, mango, pomegranate, grapefruit, orange, lemon, tomato and plum, the following questions can be asked:

Picture 5.2   *Sorting moving toys using a practical branch database*

- Is it yellow?
- Is it star-shaped?
- Does it have seeds?
- Does it have one seed?
- Has it got rough skin?
- Is it hairy?

The children will raise all these questions and many more. The database can grow with each question in the same way as a tree grows up and branches out. The resulting database can look extremely complex (see Figure 5.5) but it can be as big or small as the children want. Young children who find writing difficult can still undertake the classification, as the databases do not have to include excessive writing. Pictures of the fruit or the actual fruit can replace the names and the questions can be written by older or more able children or the teacher. Older children will be able to make more complex databases with more branches and make more use of the written word. The use of the computer can make the

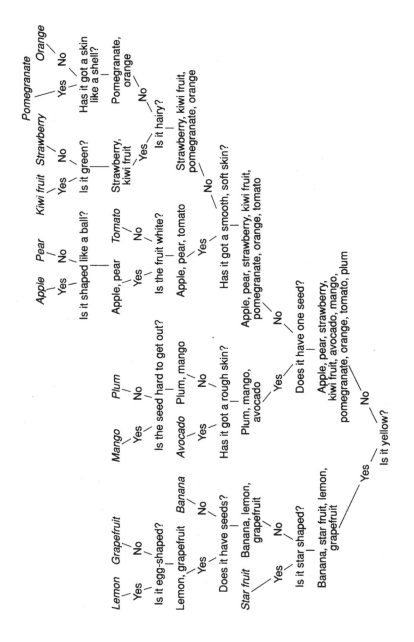

Figure 5.5 A branch database classifying a collection of fruit

procedure easier for young children. The computer will ask the children to write questions and name the fruit in each category. This can be done by more able children or the teacher with on-screen pictures and questions. The database grows quickly and can be added to by other groups of children at different times. As the computer takes you through each step you are not aware of the complexity of the database until a printout is made. Classification of some of the collections described in Chapter 2 can be made more fun in this way and can be as complex as the child or teacher wishes.

The passport used as part of the travel agent activity described in Chapter 3 (see Figure 3.3) is an example of a relational database. For the youngest or least able children, the data can be simple and pictorial. Older or more able children can collect information on a range of physical features and personal preferences. For the eldest and very able, this information could be put on to a class spreadsheet and graphs and tables can be made to show hair colour, eye colour, favourite colour, etc. The passport photographs, made using a digital camera, can be used on the graphs or tables to illustrate data more vividly for the children. Children can also raise questions, which examination of the data can attempt to answer, for example, 'Do all fair-haired children have blue eyes?', 'Are the eldest children the tallest?', or 'Can children with bigger feet jump higher?'

Some ICT can allow children to experience phenomena which otherwise would be unavailable, for example, see inside the human body, explore the solar system and observe plant growth or the life cycle of a butterfly, speeded up through time-lapse photography. Some programs contain interactive simulations, which provide opportunities to predict and hypothesize in scientific situations normally outside children's experiences. Children need to develop skills in making predictions and hypotheses, and they should not attempt an investigation in science without having the opportunity to think about possible outcomes or to develop personal theories. They should then have the opportunity, where possible, to test out their ideas, but it can be difficult to give children these opportunities in every scientific situation. For example, it is not always possible to provide opportunities for children to explore different environments and to begin to develop an understanding that observable differences in animals and plants may result from the environment in which they live. CD-ROMs and videos can enable children to explore the Arctic or a desert or a rainforest in a more real way than books. It may be that the local environment holds limited potential for observation of plants and animals; for example, it may be difficult to study aspects of rural ecosystems or classify wild flowers in an inner-city school. It may be more appropriate to study some plants and animals at a difficult or unseasonable time of year or when weather conditions are not suitable, or it may be that some activities would endanger animals and plants in the environment. Again some ICT can enable children to explore the year of a tree or see wild flowers *in situ*. Some computer simulation programs can allow children to make decisions regarding the environment, predict the outcomes of their decisions and then test them out.

ICT cannot replace first-hand experience, rather it can complement it and aid the development of scientific skills, such as observation, prediction and hypothesis. This development will not occur automatically, without practitioner interaction and skilled planning. However, ICT can be a very useful tool to help the development of scientific skills in a motivating way (see Table 5.1).

Information and communication technology can also help to motivate children when planning explorations and investigations, modifying their plans as a result of discussions and trying them out in a practical way. This involves making both qualitative and quantitative measurements. I believe that early-years children need to make qualitative observations before they are able to make sense of measurements taken using quantitative measuring devices. For example, children would need to explore the concepts of hot and cold in a qualitative way, that is by feeling water temperatures, in order to be able to conceptualize how temperature gauges, such as thermometers, work.

There are some computer data logging packages that can help young children to take qualitative measurements and make their explorations and investigations fun. Data logging is the automatic recording, storing and displaying of information received from sensors which react to changes in temperature, light level, movement and so on. The sensors can be plugged directly into the computer or into an interface and can collect data in a digital or analogue form. Digital sensors are simple switches, such as pressure mats or light gates which register an on or off state, or trigger other events. Analogue sensors include temperature and light sensors which show a gradual change from minimum to maximum levels and can record changes over time. There are a number of different data loggers available and some are very suitable for early-years children. For example, when children are exploring temperature differences some programs use colour rather than numbers with the computer screen changing colour with the temperature. These sensors can also display temperatures digitally, which is easier for children to read than the scale on traditional thermometers.

The use of temperature sensors can motivate children to explore or investigate more fully, but it is necessary to progress from qualitative data collection, either manually or on computer or both, before quantitative data can be understood. As already described, children would need to explore the concept of heat in a qualitative way, by feeling or by

Table 5.1 How information and communication technology can help the development of scientific knowledge, skills and attitudes

The advantages of using ICT in science	Considerations in the use of ICT
• Children find ICT stimulating and motivating.	• Teachers often lack confidence in using new technology. ICT can be frustrating if it is too complex for the learner.
• ICT can develop the scientific skills of observation and raising questions through the use of databases and spreadsheets.	• ICT cannot fully develop skills. Other work will always be necessary. Some databases and spreadsheets can be complex. The more sophisticated the software the more complex it may be to use.
• ICT can develop the scientific skills of observing, predicting and hypothesizing through the use of simulations and time-lapse video. They can enable children to make decisions and be practically involved in aspects of science for which this is difficult.	• ICT should not replace first-hand experiences, but complement them.
• ICT can develop the scientific skills of planning and investigating through the use of sensors and data-logging devices. This can allow children the opportunity to collect data at any time.	• Care needs to be taken in setting up the computer to avoid computer error which invalidates all data. Children's conceptual understanding will not be developed unless they are aware of what data they are collecting and why.
• ICT can develop the scientific skills of measuring through a focus on qualitative observations and the use of sensors which measure accurately.	• Children need to have experience of making qualitative observations before they can understand the quantitative measurements taken with or without a computer.
• ICT can develop the scientific skills of recording, communicating and interpreting through use of word-processing, database, and graphics packages, etc., which make recording of data more interesting and meaningful.	• Data recorded by means of ICT will only be meaningful to children if they are allowed opportunities to consider and interpret them, and to communicate their interpretations to others.
• Children's conceptual development will occur through the choice of knowledge-based software.	• ICT can aid conceptual development alongside the development of skills and attitudes. Conceptual development will only occur where children are given a variety of opportunities to work inside the concept.

using simple electronic sensors which show changes by means of colour, in order successfully to interpret data collected using temperature gauges such as thermometers. They would need to have experience of both methods of data collection in order for analysis of data collected electronically to have any meaning for them. Another motivation for the use of sensors in simple investigations is that data can be collected over a period of time, and this means that children can collect data they would not normally have access to or investigate for an extended period of time. Children could observe the temperature, light or noise levels in their classrooms over a period of time or how temperature or light affects the growth of seeds or plants over time. Using a remote sensor (one that can be used away from the computer or mains electricity) children can collect data away from the classroom and the computer. For example, using a pressure mat they can explore how many birds visit a bird table, log the temperature, light and sound levels in the school garden over a 24-hour period or the water temperature, air temperature, light and sound in the local swimming baths.

Recording and communicating are further important skills in science that can be developed in a motivating way through ICT. Of course, not all activities need to be recorded and early-years children may record in a variety of ways (pictures, talk, made products). Written recording is often the part of a scientific activity that many children find a burden. How many times have you heard the plea 'Do we *have* to write about it?' The use of ICT does reduce that burden for many children, provide opportunities for children who find writing inhibits their creativity and scientific development and it makes the recording of data more exciting for all. Children can use cassette recorders to make audio tapes of their work in the form of a radio programme or a news flash. They can use video cameras to make a TV programme. They can use photographs of their work and make a book of their science activity or a photographic display. They can use computer programs to take the drudgery out of the writing up of scientific activities and make their records look more aesthetic and professional. Graphics programs allow children to draw pictures, make plans, graphs and diagrams. Word-processing packages can help children in writing and some specialize in supporting young children or children who find writing difficult. Written work can take a variety of forms – stories, poems, factual reports or the completion of cloze procedure (sentences provided with missing words which children have to enter in the appropriate place) or worksheets produced, by the teacher, using the computer. Stories and poems are a lovely cross-curricular way for children to record and communicate their feelings in science or their ideas on some areas of science. Word processing can also help in making the children's writing look professional and in giving children pride in their work.

Tables, plans, charts and graphs can be produced from data children collect, allowing them to record their results in an organized way. These may not always be appropriate for young children as they do need physically to experience the graphical presentation of their data before feeding it into a computer. I have used simple programs to produce block graphs for Year 2 children and there are increasingly more programs that are suitable for graphical representation with younger children. Tables, plans and graphs can be used to develop interpretative skills. Graphs made during data logging in the classroom, using light, sound and temperature sensors, can tell you when the noisy and quiet times in the class are, what time it gets dark and when the teachers, caretaker and cleaners went home. Children can begin to look for patterns in the data or for anomalies such as:

- Who made the noise in the night?
- Was it a burglar or the hamster on a midnight prowl?
- What time does the boiler come on in the morning?
- Why does it get warmer in the classroom after 9.00 a.m.?
- Why is it noisy at 10.30 a.m. and 12.00 noon?

It is important that children have the opportunity to interpret their data and help to develop simple hypotheses.

Television and video together are another useful motivating force for creative science activities. They can provide a stimulating introduction to a theme or concept, encourage and develop ideas during science work and suggest further explorations and investigations. Care is needed when using the media, as with all forms of ICT and science educational books. We need to evaluate the educational worth of the programmes, ensure they are appropriate for the age of the children we teach, match our identified learning objectives and fit in with our schemes of work. We cannot justify the use of programmes in isolation with little or no follow-up work or thought about the educational justification for using them. We cannot expect that a programme will do our work in planning, evaluating and assessing, and we cannot replace practical exploration and investigation with any programme, however good. We additionally need to be careful about the context of programmes. Some appear so full of razzmatazz that, while they are obviously motivating, the educational links are somewhat smothered; they may be so entertaining that the scientific point is lost. Others seem to perpetuate beliefs about science 'which persist from popular belief and the caricatures which are perpetuated in the media and in some literature' (Harlen, 2000: 18); using the male, white, mad scientific inventor who is somehow alien to everyday life and people or provide images of science as factual, involving empirical methodology and being irrelevant to everyday life.

We need to show children that science is applicable to us all, at any age, regardless of gender, race or ability, and that science is multifaceted, creative and can be qualitative.

Creative science and art

Many of the explorations described throughout this book involve creative, thematic elements, which arise from the children's own interests, as advocated by current thinking and good practice (QCA, 2000; DfES, 2003). 'Difficult' scientific concepts can often be developed through creative, thematic, cross-curricular activities. In conjunction with a questioning approach, which encourages children to focus on the concepts involved and the skills we wish to develop, this can be very successful and help to facilitate the development of ideas and skills. There are some good creative explorations, involving science and art, but it should be remembered that creativity does not just involve the artistic and musical, but also involves thinking (see Chapter 3) and awe inspiring activities (see Chapter 4).

Young children can explore materials through art, by adding flour, salt, sand or sawdust to finger paint and recording the effect by applying to paper or making a mono-print with paper. They can also explore and investigate forces through art. There are a number of creative activities linking science and art which focus on forces. With each of these the recording is through art and the artistic result can be interpreted to focus on the forces involved. One activity investigates the patterns created by paint and sand pendulums. A paint pendulum can be made using a washing-up liquid bottle, with the bottom cut out (Figure 5.6). This can be hand-held or suspended upside down from a piece of wood bridging a gap between two tables and filled with either silver sand or liquid paint. When released the pendulum makes patterns on large sheets of paper. It is best to use dark-coloured paper for sand as it will show up better. The patterns created by different pendulums, different lengths of string and different methods of release can be investigated. While doing this children can be asked questions to encourage them to focus on the forces involved.

- What do you notice?
- How can you change the pattern?
- What do you think makes the pendulum start/stop swinging?
- When does the pendulum slow down?
- Why is the pattern different?

Figure 5.6   The paint pendulum

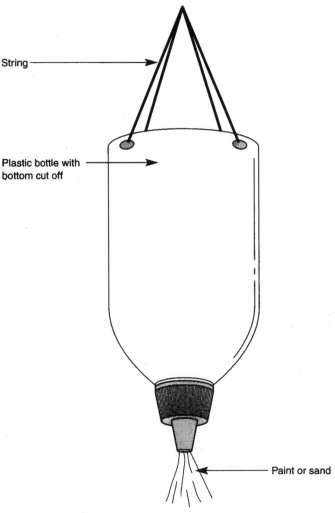

It can be a messy activity, but small groups of young children can successfully look at the forces involved; the forces which make the pendulum start swinging, stop swinging, slow down, change the pattern and change direction.

The second creative activity involves exploring and investigating the effects of dropping paint-coloured water from a pipette on to paper. The result is a 'splat'. If children look closely at these they notice a number of features about them.

Look, it's got spikes.
Mine's bigger.
This one's smoother.

The questions you ask the children can help to focus their ideas and lead to further explorations and investigations:

- How many spikes has your splat got?
- How can you make a splat with more spikes?
- Why do you think some splats are bigger than others?
- How can you make your splats bigger/smaller?
- What sort of splats do you think you will get if you let the drop fall from 1 metre/2 metres?
- What do you think makes a splat?
- Do you think your splat will look different if you use blotting paper/plastic/newspaper?
- Do you think the size of your drop will make a difference? How?

In this way further explorations can focus on the shape of the splats, the spikes coming out of the splats and how these change in number or size

Picture 5.3   *Exploring the science in splats*

with height or size of drop, the type of paper or type of liquid used. In all cases the children should be encouraged to consider the forces involved in these changes; the force which makes the drop of paint fall, how changes in the force change the shape of the splat and how you can affect the forces by changing the paper, the way you drop the paint and so on.

The third creative activity I use to focus on forces involves a paint spinner. This can be a salad spinner with a circle of card inside it and a strip of card around its sides. You can also use a large circle of card fixed to an electric motor, placed inside a box (Figure 5.7) or with a salad spinner basket, with paper inside, attached to the base. There are available commercial paint spinners and these work in a similar way to a push-down toy spinning top. You could also use all three methods and, in addition to considering the forces involved, look at comparisons between the energy sources and how they work, as well as the end results. If the spinner has sides and/or a lid this is a relatively clean activity, although without the sides it can be messy and needs care and attention. Paint can be carefully put on to the circle and the effects of centrifugal force can be seen in the resulting patterns. Children look carefully at the patterns resulting from the paint spinner and, once again, questions can focus on the forces and encourage them to explore further:

- Can you change the speed of the spinner?
- What do you think will happen if you use thicker/thinner paint?
- Do you think you will change the pattern if you use more/less paint?
- How do you think the pattern is made?
- Do you think the size/type of the paper makes a difference to the pattern?

This type of activity can develop some understanding of forces through consideration of what is making the paint drops move and make patterns, but will not develop full understanding of the forces involved. It is especially useful for developing understanding of the scientific process, allowing children to observe, predict, plan and hypothesize. All activities at this stage should be concerned with developing scientific skills and attitudes and with developing initial ideas about scientific phenomena which can be developed at a later stage. It is about experiencing and saying 'Wow look at that.' The 'wow' factor will be remembered at a later stage and better understanding of why will then begin.

The final activity looks at surface tension of water through marbling. This is an old activity used in many classrooms, although I would suggest that in most cases the science inherent in the activity is not focused upon. A few drops of oil-based ink are dropped on to a tray of water using a pipette. The oil and water do not mix and the oil floats on top of the

Figure 5.7   The paint spinner

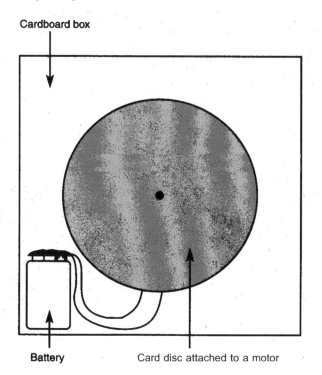

Cardboard box

Battery   Card disc attached to a motor

water. Observations of the patterns on the water can lead to simple hypotheses.

- Why do you think the ink is not mixing with the water?
- Why do you think the ink is floating on the water?
- What do you think holds the ink up?

The pattern can be captured by placing a piece of paper on top of the water and carefully lifting it off. The children can explore different colours, size of ink drops and type of paper. You can then observe what happens if you add a drop of liquid detergent to the water.

Picture 5.4   *Exploring floating and sinking through marbling*

Creative science from literature

Literature can be a good starting point and help to re-create an imaginary situation in the classroom. *The Tiny Seed* by Eric Carle (1987) can aid work in the garden centre (see Chapter 1), developing skills of observation, classification, as well as knowledge about seeds and the growth of plants. *Handa's Surprise* by Eileen Browne (1997) and *The Very Hungry Caterpillar* by Eric Carle (1970) can support exploration of a variety of fruit and/or vegetables, developing skills of observation, prediction and hypothesis. *Mr Archimedes Bath* by Pamela Allen (1986) can provide a stimulus for water play and exploring forces in water. *Stig of the Dump* by Clive King (1963), *The Selfish Giant* by Oscar Wilde (1978) and *Planet of the Monsters* by Stephen May (1985) have all provided the initial stimulus for Key Stage 1 work in science, mathematics, technology and English in a fun and motivating way.

I have used *Jim and the Beanstalk* by Raymond Briggs (1970) with Reception children to look at knowledge of the human body and the similarities and differences between them and others (age, size and physical characteristics). I produced a story sack containing:

- the book
- Giant and Jim puppets
- a wig
- some false teeth
- a tape measure
- a climbing Jim (see climbing man, see Figure 5.4)
- a collection of glasses
- some gold coins
- writing paper and envelopes

and used it to help tell the children the story of Jim and Beanstalk. We stopped at points in the story to look at physical differences between the giant and Jim, such as their age, size, hair, eyes, teeth and personality (see also Johnston and Herridge, 2004).

Picture 5.5   *Exploring similarities and differences using a story sack of* Jim and the Beanstalk (Briggs, 1973)

Afterwards the children used the story sack to retell the story and describe the physical differences between Jim and the Giant and wrote thank-you letters to the giant from Jim. In this way, they were developing language, literacy and measuring skills, as well as knowledge about the human body and the similarities and differences between humans. Older children could use the story as a stimulus for making a wig for the giant, focusing on materials suitable for the hair and the adhesives used to glue the wig as well as size and shape and length. They can also look at light, lenses and vision by making a set of glasses for the giant and consider dental hygiene as well as materials suitable for making false teeth. The advantage of this type of working can be that the activity has obvious meaning to the children and they are more likely to be creative in their own right.

Another example of a literature stimulus is *Mrs Lather's Laundry* by Alan Ahlberg (1981) which can provide opportunities to look at everyday experiences in a different way. Children can use solutions of detergent to create bubbles of varying types. A variety of bubble wands, blowers and bubble-making devices can produce bubbles of different sizes and even bubbles of the same shape from different-shaped beginnings! Different types of washing-up liquid and bubble bath can be used to create the best, biggest, strongest, longest-lasting or most colourful bubbles.

Mrs Lather's laundry can be created in the classroom, and while the children can explore the bubbles, resulting in scientific development, they can also be involved in other curriculum development. Language development can occur through play interaction. Mathematical development can occur through the laundry's financial transactions and even historical explorations in researching how washing has changed through the years. An added stimulus could be a visit to a local laundry or dry-cleaner, and this is likely to lead to understanding of the part science and technology play in society, through exploration of the laundry as a workplace, the use of resources in the laundry and the disposal of laundry waste and the energy cost of laundry services.

From initial observations of bubbles, as part of Mrs Lather's laundry, children could explore light and colour, forces acting on the bubbles and different bubble solutions and water temperature. The resulting development in science could be in terms of the following concepts, knowledge, skills and attitudes, although I should stress that others could equally be developed. I should also add that it would be most unlikely that all these areas would be developed in one child through one activity.

Concept: Light
Knowledge:
- I can see that bubbles are coloured (light is made up of colours which can be seen in bubbles as a result of interference effects of light on the bubble film).
- I can see my own face in the bubble (light can be reflected in bubbles).
- I can see myself upside down and the right way up in the bubble (different surfaces of the bubble can result in different reflective images and you can see your image reflected in the concave and convex surfaces of the bubbles simultaneously).

Concept: Forces
Knowledge:
- When I blow bubbles, they fall to the ground, float away or burst (forces are acting on the bubbles).
- I can see the colours in the bubble swirling around (the forces acting on the bubbles can be seen in the swirling of the colours).
- My bubbles are always spherical whatever the shape of the bubble maker or wand.

Concept: Materials
Knowledge:
- I found out that different bubble mixtures produce bubbles of differing strengths, size and some can last longer.

Concept: Energy
Knowledge:
- I found out that warm water makes better bubbles (water temperature will affect quantity of the bubbles produced).

Skills

• Observation	– I can see colours in my bubble.
	– The colours are swirling around.
	– Bubbles are always spherical.
• Raising questions	– How big can I make a bubble?
	– What makes the biggest bubble?
	– How can I make my bubble stronger?
• Planning	– How can I find out if the bubble mixture is stronger?
	– If I use a torch I think I will find out if the light goes through a bubble.
• Exploring and investigating	– Which bubble solution is best for making bubbles?
	– What temperature is best for making bubbles?
• Predicting	– What will happen if I blow a square bubble?

- Hypothesizing
  - – How long will this bubble last?
  - – Why are bubbles always spherical?
  - – Why do bubbles burst?
- Communicating
  and interpreting
  - – I can tell you which bubble solution is best.
  - – I know why I can see my face in a bubble.

Attitudes
- Curiosity
  - – I want to find out why the bubbles have different colours.
  - – I am interested in how you can make a bubble last longer.
- Open-mindedness
  - – I will try this and see what happens.
  - – I think the bubbles may last longer because the mixture is thicker.
  - – I thought this bubble would have more colours in but it has not.
- Critical reflection
  - – I could make bubble mixture better by adding less water.
  - – I could change my investigation to make it better.

Picture 5.6 *Exploring lathers from a stimulus of* Mrs Lather's Laundry (Alberg, 1981)

What are the features of creative science activities?

Creative science activities can take a variety of different forms and have a number of different features. First, the context is likely to be novel and imaginative. A relevant contextual framework is considered to be an important aspect of effective early-years teaching (QCA, 2000) and early-years science teaching (de Bóo, 2004), although this can be achieved through either a topic or subject-specific method. This may involve creating a whole environment in which to work such as a play or discovery area or immersion in a theme or book. It may involve using a ready-made environment such as computer simulation. It may involve the creative use of resources or technology, such as use of the computer to add a dimension to an investigation. It may involve using or looking at everyday phenomena from a different perspective, such as looking at splats or magic tricks.

Second, the work is likely to be cross-curricular in nature. This has the advantage of making the activity meaningful by not separating the curriculum or knowledge into discrete compartments which bear little relation to the outside world. Of course, in the Foundation Stage of Learning knowledge and understanding of the world is not compartmentalized, although practice at Key Stage 1 can be separate, different disciplines in an artificial way. Cross-curricular learning, in conjunction with a suitable context, provides clarity of meaning for the children involved. The activity will involve the whole child in a meaningful way and this will improve motivation for learning in general.

Third, the work is likely to be more exploratory and take into account the children's own ideas for further development, modification or change. In this way it will develop skills, concepts, knowledge and attitudes in a coherent way. It will probably cover a larger number of areas of development, as described in the example of Mrs Lather's laundry, and be better differentiated to meet children's individual needs.

Fourth, the activities are likely to be pupil-generated to a larger degree. Teacher support and guidance are necessary for success, but not teacher dependence. From an initial stimulus and through the provision of resources, which the children can use to explore and raise questions, simple explorations and investigations can be planned by the children to answer their questions.

There is a need to plan well to enable the children to follow their own investigative pathways, but there is also a need to be flexible to allow new and unforeseen pathways to be explored. In exploring and investigating bubbles the teacher or the children may choose to explore the concepts of light, materials, forces or energy, developing knowledge in the ways described earlier, but it is equally possible that other unexpected concepts and knowledge will be explored. I have often been amazed by the ingenuity of learners in looking at something old from a completely new perspective. I have discovered this most often when exploring ice balloons, where new areas for exploration are uncovered each time I teach it. The added advantage of this is that teaching remains exciting and innovative and I remain enthusiastic despite visiting an activity on numerous occasions. There are issues here related to the teacher's role in decision-making about curriculum organization and teaching strategies, and these will be further explored in Chapter 6.

More traditional activities differ in a number of ways. They are more likely to be initiated and directed by the teacher, to consider only one small aspect of science, to relate only to the science curriculum, to have a limited time-span and to be less well matched to the differentiated needs of the child. I am not advocating teaching solely through creative science activities; neither am I suggesting that more traditional teacher-initiated and structured activities cannot be creative in their own way. A balance in the provision of activities is always desirable and is more likely to achieve quality learning. I am also not suggesting that creative science activities as described in this chapter are not themselves without problems.

The dangers of creative science activities

The difficulties teachers face in providing creative science activities need to be identified and considered in order for teachers to make informed decisions as to whether to provide such activities at all or whether to proceed with caution. In many ways the way to evaluate creative science is to 'have a go and see', and there is little anyone can do to replace first-hand evaluation. However, it is an advantage for teachers to know the dangers before they embark on what may be a new venture.

Organizational difficulties are recognized to be a major obstacle in the path of creativity. We obviously want our children to have quality experiences but we do not wish to provide stimulating science activities at the expense of quality learning or classroom sanity. We want our children to have exciting experiences but not to disregard individual safety. We want to enjoy our teaching and learning experiences but we do wish to consider the needs of others in school: other classes, teaching staff, the cleaning staff and the caretaker. Whole-class experiential and literature-based explorations can pose organizational difficulties, but not all creative science activities have to be as adventurous as some described here. Smaller-scale play activities, small-group work and activities that are partially structured to provide quality teaching and learning opportunities can be a good start, and ensure a smooth-running but enjoyable classroom environment.

Cumming (1995) succeeded in providing a stimulating set of experiences for her class of reception and Year 1 children through the theme of Humpty Dumpty. Her activities were, in the main, teacher-initiated and included looking at forces in the structure and shape of eggs, looking at materials through the cooking of eggs and growth by using egg shells to grow seeds. I have used 'Hickory Dickory Dock' in a similar way, providing structure in my organization. As our teaching confidence develops we can attempt more experiential ways of learning but still retain the structure and support we need.

The debate as to whether creative science activities that are cross-curricular in nature can provide effective coverage of the National Curriculum has been around for some years and is likely to remain as an important consideration. However, creative teaching and learning is not a finite art and can be achieved through a variety of approaches. We can be creative in the provision of science activities using a variety of teaching and learning methods. Creative science does not have to be cross-curricular but it does need to be satisfying for the children and teachers involved. Curriculum coverage can be obtained through creative exploration, but the difficulty remains of monitoring for the diversity in coverage of creative, flexible activities. Additionally, forward planning can be disrupted as children move along unexpected avenues. The solution is not 'to put all your eggs in one basket' but to plan a variety of creative teaching methods, some of which allow children to take more responsibility for their own learning while others are structured to provide the experiences we know they need to fulfil the National Curriculum demands and their own development. In this way the monitoring of learning becomes no more complex than it is in any other classroom environment.

Assessment of learning can be another difficulty that teachers face. It is especially so if we allow assessment to drive the curriculum rather than use assessment to inform us of the children's needs and to help in planning differentiated activities. If we become so focused on summative assessments, the result will be an arid curriculum with little creativity and poor motivation and development on the part of the children. In the creative classroom assessment can still take place, and we can hopefully move away from assessing the work children have undertaken to assessing the individual achievements of children. Assessment as an individual process becomes no more difficult in a creative activity than it does in any other activity. Remember, though, that assessment should not be allowed to determine teaching but should support it.

What may be more of a problem is the actual learning which occurs.

Creative science does not mean that we do not assess the children's needs and plan accordingly. Neither does it mean that we should not have specific learning objectives which we set out to achieve. It does mean that we need to be more skilful in facilitating children's learning. We need to ensure that there is some real learning involved in the activity and not simply a fun set of experiences for children. I have seen classroom activities judged on the basis of the fun element rather than the learning element. Learning should be fun, it should be motivating, it should be creative, but it should also be meaningful. Practitioners need to identify the learning inherent in an activity and assess its development.

The final problem with creative science is concerned with the message about science that we are projecting. We want children to realize that science is fun and creative, but we also want children to get a full picture of the nature of science. We do not want science to appear completely serious, and irrelevant to everyday life, but neither do we want it to be considered frivolous. In planning science activities, we do need to be careful about the messages that we are giving to children about the nature of science and ensure that they have a balanced picture. If we provide relevant, meaningful and motivating experiences for children they will have fun and develop the desire to understand the scientific principles underpinning the experiences.

Summary

- Good science teaching can be fun and effective and creative science can be a reality.
- Creative science activities can take a variety of forms. No one way is better at everything than another.
- Creative science explorations can be very effective at developing the whole child in a coherent, cross-curricular way.
- While creative science activities are enjoyable and entertaining it is important to remember the learning objectives involved.
- In planning creative science explorations there is a need to consider the messages about science we are conveying.

6

Creative teaching and provision

Creative learning requires creative teaching and provision, for as W. B. Yeats identified 'education is not the filling of a pail but the lighting of a fire'. Creative teaching and provision in science has three essential elements; it should be practical, memorable and interactive. In Chapter 2 I discussed the different types of practical work at length and concluded that explorations are the most suitable for children in the early years. In Chapter 4 I focused on the importance of attitudes and how memorable science is important, that is science which inspires and motivates children and supports scientific development. Throughout, I have discussed the importance of children interacting with scientific phenomena, each other and adults. In this Chapter I put these important factors together for effective teaching and learning in context. In particular I will look at how the practitioner can develop creative learning contexts and provide creative learning experiences.

The role of the practitioner

The role of the practitioner in early scientific development is an essential part of the learning process. This role will reflect the practitioner's philosophy on development and learning in general, and teaching and learning in early science in particular. A scientific philosophy develops as a result of scientific understanding, personal experiences and reflection on those understandings and experiences. School and home science experiences, practitioner training and professional experiences will all be of influence here. Practitioners enter the learning profession with their own personal beliefs about development and education which include ideas on the professionalism of the practitioner, the different roles within the learning environment, the value and nature of early science education, the aim of science education and what good early science development and teaching involves. Sometimes these beliefs are limited in breadth and depth (Johnston *et al.*, 1998; Johnston and Ahtee, 2005) but they are likely to reflect the beliefs within the wider society.

We only need to listen to news broadcasts or read the newspapers to realize that it is not just practitioners who have quite firm philosophies on education; we all have. Hardly a week goes by without someone saying what nurseries and schools should do or what their responsibilities are. All of society has an opinion on the purpose of early provision, what it should include and how providers should achieve the numerous demands made upon them. It is understandable that all of society should have an opinion about education. Individuals within society have all experienced education, and this experience has enabled them to formulate firm ideas about it. Unfortunately these experiences also lead individuals to believe they are knowledgeable about all aspects of educational provision even if their experiences have been limited and their knowledge does not give them a broad overview of education and wider development.

There are many cultural differences in childhood and educational philosophies (see Berk, 2003) and practitioners need to be inclusive of all different philosophies to avoid alienating children (Harlen, 2000). Cultural differences in philosophies of science development and education will also be reflected within the teaching profession (Johnston *et al.*, 1998) and the wider society. Within Europe there is considerable difference between educational philosophy and practice reflecting historical cultural and philosophical differences (see also Chapter 1). In England and Wales, our approaches before 1991 had developed out of an established philosophy of teaching, historical research and observation of practice. With the introduction of the National Curriculum, we moved from very child-centred early-years educational practice to more curriculum-focused practice, especially at Key Stage 1. At the same time many European countries (for example, Finland, Russia, Bosnia, Macedonia) began to develop a more child-centred approach from a traditionally rigid curriculum-centred approach. However, with the introduction of a skills-focused curriculum in the Foundation Stage and an endorsement of principles for young children based on good practice (QCA, 2000), early-years education has gradually reversed the trend and the effects can be seen not only in the Foundation Stage and Key Stage 1 but also (but less commonly) in some Key Stage 2 classes.

Within the school, individual philosophies are shared and mixed, and the result is a school philosophy that should be an eclectic compromise between individual differences. Individuals within the school need to debate their beliefs and come to a common understanding or a common belief about their educational aims and objectives and how they can best be achieved. Working together inevitably means that some individual ideas will not fit the school philosophy, but it is essential that practitioners work towards a common aim and have a common understanding of how that aim can best be achieved. This may mean that individuals need to modify their philosophies, or shelve aspects of them until changes in school, staff or educational climate make them more generally acceptable. Major differences in beliefs and practices can lead to discontinuity for children, although continuity should not be mistaken for consistency, which Oscar Wilde said 'is the last refuge of the unimaginative'. The most advantageous aspect of the National Curriculum and Foundation Curriculum is that for the first time in national education in England and Wales, all children should receive similar science experiences during their early years. However, the experiences of learning may be quite different and, while it is important that children develop the ability to learn in a variety of situations, it is important also that children who have these experiences do not have their development impaired or slowed by discontinuity. I am not suggesting that all provision should be identical or even similar, but I am indicating that providers need to plan not only for the science content, but also for the method of delivery. In my early years of teaching, little debate about the teacher's role, curriculum organization and learning preferences occurred, and I am aware that my own teaching did little to provide continuity for the children. Within school, children could move from teacher-directed learning to more flexible learning situations and then to didactic teaching situations, and there was no consideration of how they would benefit from these teaching and learning situations, what messages about science were being given or how effective their scientific development was. The effect of this discontinuity on the development of generic learning and social skills and emotional development, including attitudes, is great, as these are often unplanned and poorly developed aspects of development and learning.

Most science policies (or policies on how the key area of Knowledge and Understanding of the World can be developed) reflect the need to meet the aims of either the Foundation Curriculum or the National Curriculum and contain statements to that effect, but they also indicate the science experiences which will achieve these aims, how science should be taught and the underlying philosophy of the providers. They indicate whether science should

- be incidental or planned;
- be part of a theme;
- be a distinctly separate part of the curriculum;
- be planned rigidly;
- meet certain objectives at different stages;
- stem from the children's explorations;
- be guided by the practitioner.

Continuity implies consistency in aims, values and expectations. Practitioners working together should have a shared philosophy of education and be working towards a common educational goal. Continuity does not imply uniformity of experience. Practitioners' individual creativity and style should not be affected by continuity. It also implies good professional relationships with managers, teachers, nursery nurses, classroom assistants, who can all effectively utilize their professional and different expertise towards a common goal. This continuity can be achieved through an effective learning partnership or team-work approach to policy, planning, teaching and learning. This could involve joint policy decisions and sharing of philosophy, goals and modes of delivery. It could involve shared planning for one year, one key stage, or throughout the nursery or school. It could involve the sharing of ideas for activities and effective practitioner styles, it could involve working to strengths and expertise throughout a year or the whole school or it could include shared practice. We need to remember that all adults concerned in the learning partnership have different strengths and expertise. Practitioners trained in childcare have great knowledge about child development and health, qualified teachers have knowledge about the learning process and teaching, carers have depth of understanding about individual children and all adults have individual interests and expertise. My own teaching experience has been diverse. I have taught in situations where there was little continuity and few agreed aims, but also in others where team work was highly valued in order to meet the schools' aims. In one school I was responsible for the planning and teaching of the whole science curriculum; in another year, groups planned together and team teaching ensured best use of curriculum expertise and provided an element of staff development. Whatever the school's way of working, full commitment was essential in order to achieve continuity in science teaching and learning. Practitioners needed to agree on a philosophy on science education and find out both the children's and their colleagues' working preferences and plan to accommodate these and the goals set by the relevant curriculum in science. Discussion and planning are the keys to effective scientific development and teachers need to plan

- for the practitioner's role;
- for the children's learning;
- for the context of learning;
- for the organization of effective learning,

and these may involve different demands at different stages in the early years.

Planning for the practitioner's role

The role of the practitioner is important as children develop better if care is consistent and staff turnover is low. This has implications for Advanced Skills Teachers (ASTs) and job-share situations in the early years of development, where children's insecurity in the setting and a slower rate of development can be attributed to a lack of consistency of care. Decisions about the role of the practitioner are important in the development of a motivating learning environment. There have been a number of attempts to categorize the role of the practitioner in the early years (Rowland, 1984; Osborne and Freyberg, 1985; Dean, 2001) and in primary science (Harlen, 2000) and the resulting teaching and learning styles (Johnston, 1996). A child-centred approach to teaching and learning is generally advocated (QCA, 2000; DfES, 2003) but, hopefully, we would not use one approach exclusively. We should review the balance between direct and indirect teaching approaches, rather than adopt a mechanistic approach; 'a repetition of repetitions' (D. H. Lawrence). With each approach the practitioner's role will differ, but I believe that the main feature of the role remains the same, that is, that the practitioner is a facilitator of learning rather than an imparter of knowledge. This role hinges on the belief that teaching and learning are not passive experiences in which a 'teacher' imparts knowledge to the learner, who is then able to use or apply that learning in everyday life. Teaching and learning are active experiences involving significant interactions between the learner and others who influence development (see Figure 4.4). This idea is not new and is embodied in many of the already identified teaching and learning approaches. This view of the practitioner also embodies the teaching roles identified by Osborne and Freyberg (1985), of motivator, diagnostician, guide, innovator, experimenter and researcher, although the teacher as a role model for learning is very important (Gardner, 1991; Dean, 2001). Consideration of some teaching and learning approaches in primary science can help us to identify these roles. In looking at these approaches we should remember that a good practitioner does not rely on one approach, but uses a variety and that different approaches have different uses and advantages, with in each case, the most important factor being adult interaction (Siraj-Blatchford *et al.*, 2002; Riley, 2003).

An instructional approach

This approach involves the practitioner as an imparter of knowledge, and while it cannot alone develop skills and conceptual understanding, it does have a place in early years development. During a scientific exploration children may need some guidance, direction or even instruction to enable them to succeed.

While exploring fabrics, Darren and Paul decided to find out which material was the warmest. The idea for exploration was decided by the teacher but they decided what focus their investigation would take. They needed help in the planning of an investigation to ensure that it would be successful. This help took the form of listening to their ideas and guiding them towards consideration of the variables involved. An initial idea was to make a glove out of each material and see which glove was the warmest. The teacher helped them to make a mitten with each piece of material which they put on their hands in the cold playground. They made qualitative judgements about the warmth of the materials, but some were difficult to separate and there was disagreement between the boys. The teacher suggested that they measured how warm the mittens kept something by using a thermometer. They then decided to put something hot into each mitten and take the temperature. The teacher suggested they cover a plastic cup containing warm water with each mitten. Before they could do this the children needed some instruction on how to use a thermometer, and guidance on how and when to take the temperatures.

This investigation was initiated by the children, guided by the teacher and then needed some specific teaching to ensure its successful outcome. The teacher's role changed throughout the activity from motivator and guide (Osborne and Freyberg, 1985) to instructor (Rowland, 1984). Some instruction or prompting is necessary in every exploration and investigation with young children. Sometimes it is to ensure the success of the activity, sometimes to show the use of scientific equipment, and sometimes it is to ensure the safe handling of living things.

We also use more instructional teaching methods in 'carpet' or 'reflective' time with young children, often at the beginning and end of sessions. This time is of great use in setting tasks, motivating the children, organizing the activities, discussing ideas and interpreting from activities.

It is also a time when the role of the practitioner becomes more instructional and indeed instructional whole-class teaching has been found (Ofsted, 2003: 6) to be *dominated by closed questions, brief answers and relatively little extended interaction,* despite the interactive pedagogy advocated by whole-class strategies (DfEE, 1998 and 1999a). The children may need instructions as to how to behave, how to use resources and what the expected outcome is. It may be that one group of children become guides and instructors for the other children by describing their explorations and ideas and helping other children to build upon their work. The hard task for any practitioner is knowing when to be instructional and when not to be. In observations of adults interacting with children, I have noticed some interesting trends regarding the teaching role. Inexperienced student teachers and parents tend to take on the instructional role to a greater extent and 'teach' the children. They appear constrained by their lack of confidence in science and their limited understanding of the nature of science. There is a body of scientific knowledge which needs to be imparted to the child. The teacher/adult is expected to have access to this body of knowledge and can be an 'authoritative instructor' (Rowland, 1981). More experienced teachers, and student teachers with greater scientific understanding and confidence in the classroom, tend to be less didactic and instructional and take on the role of the teacher as motivator and guide, spending considerably less time in passive instruction. This occurs as their confidence and experience grow.

Picture 6.1   *Using carpet time for instruction*

A discovery approach

Inherent in the discovery approach to learning in science is the desire to provide a motivating environment in which children learn through exploration. Discovery learning was very popular in the 1960s and 1970s, powerfully advocated by the Plowden Report (DES, 1967) and incorporated into primary pedagogy, although they recognized that it was often misunderstood and meant different things to different people. The narrow view of discovery science is that children take on the role of scientists and make new discoveries for themselves. The danger here is that they may not discover anything or that they are looking to see what the hidden agenda of the teacher is. I believe that it has an important place in early years scientific development and advocate a discovery approach in science where 'initial curiosity, often stimulated by the environment the teacher provides, leads to questions and to a consideration of what questions it is sensible to ask and how to find the answers' (DES, 1967: 242). This approach should build upon children's prior experiences (QCA, 2000) so they discover scientific ideas by exploring new phenomena or revisiting old experiences and most importantly discovering that learning is 'an enjoyable and challenging experience' (DfES, 2000: 29). An effective discovery approach is one where,

- the child is central to the learning;
- children discover things about the world around them, which stem from their own initial curiosity;
- children construct their own understandings from the experience of discovery, as well as develop important skills and attitudes;
- teachers support and encourage children to ensure that their discovery is meaningful to them;
- teachers utilize knowledge about the children as learners (e.g. Gardner, 1983) and pedagogical theory and practice to provide an excellent learning environment. (See Johnston, 2004.)

Discovery can be very motivating for children and it does not have to be unguided. It can be focused around learning objectives by providing specific resources, posing challenges and questions, which support the development of planned learning objectives, which if shared with the children provides them with more ownership of their learning and has a better chance of being successful. However, a discovery approach can also be successful if the learning aims and objectives are focused but less specific, and the practitioner takes the lead from the child, responding to their needs. One discovery activity I have used stems from the 'discovery box'. I have a collection of boxes, plastic tubs and tins of different shapes and sizes and each one contains different objects. One may contain a collection of different springs, another some feathers, another some leaves and another some magnets and some paper clips. I use these boxes in a number of ways. We can play a guessing game to see if the children can guess what is in the box (developing skills of observation and prediction). They may use contextual clues such as the shape or size of the box or what it was produced for (eggs, margarine, chocolates). They may use their senses and weigh or feel the box or shake it and listen to the sound inside. Once they have opened the box and removed the contents they can explore them and ask questions about them. The avenues for discovery are varied and although each box will probably have limited scope (for example, springs will lead to work on forces) I have been surprised by the diversity of explorations. With an assortment of feathers, children can explore their structure, using magnifiers or a computer microscope to look closely at them or projecting them or part of them on to a screen (focusing on materials and their properties). They can also look at how they fall through the air, comparing them with how other objects fall (with a focus on forces). I have seen children look at the patterns on feathers or see how good different feathers are for painting or writing and so the focus changes to uses of materials.

The role of the practitioner in a discovery approach is changeable. They can be motivator and innovator (Osborne and Freyberg, 1985) in providing resources and a motivating force to encourage learning. They are also responsible for guiding the children's learning to ensure that they are able to explore effectively, raise questions which can be explored further and make sense of their discoveries. The practitioner has an important role in deciding the correct way to support individuals, assessing their level of need and ability, not letting them 'flounder too long or too helplessly' (DES, 1967: 242) and supporting them by thoughtful questioning. Practitioners in the Foundation Stage often do this instinctively but sometimes we lose sight of the individual in our curriculum-focused compulsory primary education. This was illustrated to me by an experience when student teachers set up a discovery learning experience for Year 3 children. I set up a workbench with a toolbox and a collection of tools, saws, drills, drill bits, sandpaper, nails, hammers, screws, screwdrivers, rawlplugs, etc. (Johnston and Herridge, 2004). The children were encouraged to explore but asked to sort out the items and tidy the workbench. In doing this activity, the children were sorting the items according to their physical properties and use. Each child was able to choose their own criteria for sorting and all achieved the objectives well, tidying the workbench and sorting the items. One child realized that different screw heads needed different types of screwdrivers and he began to look at the door hinges and other screws in the classroom for different

Picture 6.2   *Discovering the properties of materials by sorting the toolbox in Year 3*

types of screws used. Another child began to look at the different purposes of screws and nails and consider why screws might be used rather than nails. These children were making different discoveries from an initial open-ended introduction, with focused objectives. For such an activity to be successful, I needed to provide the correct mix of support, encouragement and time for the individual learners and not 'over direct' them or give them insufficient time to engage in the activity. However, the student teachers and newly qualified class teacher were much more instructional in their approach to the detriment of both behaviour and motivation of some children.

A problem-solving approach

Problem-solving provides a good link with science and technology in the classroom. It can also provide a motivating context for children's learning. The problem of which glove is the warmest (see below) is especially motivating when it is a problem initiated by the children from their own explorations. Problems can also be set by the practitioner but care needs to be taken to ensure that such problems are motivating for the children and appear to have a real purpose.

While problem-solving can be a motivating link between primary science and technology, it can also create a dilemma about the form and purpose of science and technology in the primary classroom. Primary science can be described as developing scientific concepts, skills and attitudes through practical activities, whereas primary technology, in part, can be described as the application of some scientific concepts and skills through practical activity such as problem-solving. The dilemma occurs because in the primary classroom children are often undertaking both activities simultaneously and because, in such a situation, scientific development may be limited. Children may be set a problem to solve such as which type of paper will make the strongest tower. They may successfully plan a problem-solving investigation to make towers using different papers and test them fairly. They could be following the scientific process, and from their investigation they could solve the problem and decide which paper made the strongest tower, but there may have been little development of their scientific concepts and knowledge. Such an activity will 'involve the application of scientific ideas but perhaps not the development of these ideas if the activity stops at the point of solving the problem' (Harlen, 1992: 47).

Characteristics of problem-solving include:

- motivating practical activities;
- challenges to children's understanding;
- the development of skills and attitudes as well as understanding;
- interaction, with children interacting with ideas, resources, each other and adults;
- cross-curricular activities;
- supporting the more creative and technological learners;
- being time-consuming.

A good problem-solving activity would start from the children's interests. In the early years, this can occur during play/exploratory activities, structured by teacher interaction and questioning. Problem-solving in the sand and water can occur by asking children 'Can you make this float/sink?' or 'Can you build a big sand tower?' While children are playing with construction toys, the practitioner can suggest that they make a duplo bridge between two tables or ask if they can make a tall tower/long wall? As children develop, the problems can move from the familiar and exploratory and become more specific and challenging, although it is important that the level of challenge is correct. Too great and the children become frustrated, too little and they become bored. Challenge is a great motivator. These problem-solving activities can be made more difficult by the complexity of the challenge, the context in which they are set and the level of conceptual understanding needed to solve the problem. They can be challenged to make a plasticine boat and see how many marbles they can float in it. They can make a climbing person (see Picture 5.1) and solve the problem of how they can get the person to climb down the string. They can use mirrors to enable them to see round corners or make a periscope.

The practitioner's role would be to guide the children, defining an initial problem or initiating the problem with guidance from the children. Some guidance or instruction might be needed to enable the problem-solving to continue. However, if the problem-solving pathways had already been defined, the role would be more instructional. The problem with predefining the problem-solving pathway is that ownership and motivation may be lost and possible learning limited. A more guided role would allow for greater motivation and subsequent learning. A third role which could be adopted within a problem-solving approach is that of flexible interactor, where the teacher interacts with the children, solving the problem with them and asking questions which will focus on the scientific learning in the activity, ensuring that the children's scientific development is forwarded.

A focused approach

This approach to learning can take a number of forms. A focused investigation would have a specific scientific aim or focus. This may be initiated by the practitioner alone or in conjunction with the children. It may be decided that the scheme of work in science should focus on the human body. Activities are planned with this focus in mind, taking into consideration any previous work on the human body and the requirements of the curriculum. A focused approach can also arise out of exploration, with children observing phenomena and raising questions for further exploration and investigation. These questions can then be sorted by the teacher who decides a focus for the work, or by the teacher and children who jointly decide the focus for exploration and investigation. This approach (see Table 6.1) contains elements of Harlen's (2000) and Faire and Cosgrove's (1988) 'interactive teaching' model, Osborne and Freyberg's (1985) 'generative learning' model, and the 'constructivist learning' model of the Children's Learning in Science Project CLISP (Scott, 1987) and the SPACE Project CRIPSAT, 1986–90 (Osborne *et al.*, 1992). The focus can emerge or be modified from the children's interests and questions raised, ideas and previous knowledge or from interaction between interests and ideas. The practitioner's role is as a motivator and interactor, encouraging and motivating the children and interacting with their ideas and interests, to forward their scientific development.

Table 6.1 Models of teaching and learning

Interactive teaching (Harlen, 2000; Faire and Cosgrove, 1988)	Generative learning (Osborne and Freyberg, 1985)	Constructivist learning (Scott, 1987)
• Preparation • 'Before' views of children • Exploratory activities • Children's questions • Investigations • 'After' views of children • Reflection	• Preliminary phase • Focus phase • Challenge phase • Application	• Orientation • Elicitation of ideas • Restructuring of ideas • Application of ideas • Review change in ideas

If focusing on the human body, the practitioner may research the concept and decide what type of activities would be appropriate. They would then undertake some exploratory activities to ascertain the children's ideas and what specific activities would support development or how to adapt activities to suit individual needs. One class of Reception and Year 1 children showed considerable differences when working in this area. Most children could identify the external parts of the body (hand, foot, head, arm, etc.), although some needed more support, achieved by

Picture 6.3   *Build-a-body game*

Picture 6.4   *Children focused on the human body in their exploration*

playing a 'build a body game'. These can be made by taking an outline of a body (A4 size) with the arms, legs, head and trunk cut off and numbered and with the body part labelled on the reverse side. Using a die the children can build one body by choosing the relevant body part for the number thrown and reading the label. This will help to build up the children's vocabulary and understanding of the external parts of the body.

Some children were ready to explore the major organs in the body and drew around themselves making a chalk outline, then adding the heart, lungs, stomach and brain and labelling them.

An exploratory approach

An exploratory approach can be looked upon as a form of discovery learning in which the practitioner and child negotiate an experience for the child, which is later evaluated by both of them (Rowland, 1984). I prefer to consider this as an approach that utilizes the best aspects of all approaches in an attempt not to 'throw out the baby with the bathwater'. An exploratory approach may contain aspects from all the approaches described above and be very appropriate for the younger learner.

The practitioner's role is varied throughout the learning activity. It may begin with some 'carpet time' where the practitioner as a motivator stimulates the children and encourages their explorations. The children will then have opportunities to explore a range of phenomena with the practitioner acting as a guide, helping the children to observe and raise questions which can be further explored or investigated. The practitioner may then act as a convener, assembling the children and making sense of their ideas for further exploration and investigation. The practitioner may decide to group children together on the basis of their ideas or needs, or focus the children's ideas to enable them to undertake a specific learning pathway. It may mean that the practitioner needs to take on the role of instructor, in giving the children specific instructions on how to use a piece of equipment, or how their exploration or investigation would best proceed. During the next stage of exploration and investigation, the practitioner would continue as a motivator, but would also take on the role of interactor, asking questions to extend the children's thinking or encourage the development of their skills. Finally, the practitioner would draw together the emerging ideas and hypotheses resulting from the activity and take on the role of convener in order to disseminate ideas and challenge misconceptions.

In an effective exploratory approach to teaching and learning science the practitioner would plan for his/her part in the teaching and learning process. They would share their philosophy of education with colleagues, decide on a school philosophy and aims, plan for continuity of teaching and learning within the school and plan his/her role in the teaching and learning process. They would ensure that they provide the best balance of exploration, focus, discovery and instruction and sufficient time given to support development and also support behaviour. However, this does not mean the adult leads the child through the learning. The importance of the role of the practitioner in supporting conceptual understanding has been recognized by Vygotsky (1962) who identified the need for sensitive interaction and the creation of a zone of proximal development, whereby the child and an expert other (teacher, other child, adult) interact in a joint activity. The practitioner would be careful to ensure that the child is active and that they do not dominate interactions; they would give children the space they need to develop independently and support as required.

Our role as practitioner can have an important influence on motivation and behaviour. Often a didactic approach which controls and instructs children and does not provide balance in teaching and learning can be ineffective in developing behaviour as well as understandings, skills and attitudes. We can often have greater control over behaviour and learning, by being less controlling. This was evident from this work with the workbench, as described above, when one boy, with behavioural difficulties, responded well to the activity and spent a considerable amount of time sorting all the different sized rawlplugs (about six different sizes) into different compartments of the toolbox and labelling them carefully with a drymarker. Dominating learning situations is also not an effective way to support learning as shown by the quiet child in the garden-centre play described in Chapter 1.

Many practitioners appear to be concerned about issues of coverage, control, safety and learning and these will often dictate the approach used. The National Curriculum contains an enormous amount of material and teachers have always been concerned with covering the content. One solution is to impart knowledge in a more instructional approach, as this takes less time than exploration and discovery approaches. This solution can also appear to solve the problem of reaching targets, thus providing control over the children's learning and ensuring safety. It is however a deceptive solution, especially in science education, as quality learning occurs through teaching approaches which engage and interest children (Hidi and Harackiewicz, 2000). However, research into science in the early years (BERA, 2003: 32) indicates that practitioners are 'meeting the needs of young children for discovery and hands-on activity'.

Planning for children's learning

Planning and preparation are essential prerequisites for effective teaching and learning. In many ways the plans are less important than the process of planning for as Dwight Eisenhower said 'I have always found that plans are useless, but planning is indispensable'.

Learning implies there is a gap between children's existing ideas and the ideas we aim for them to develop. One of the practitioner's roles is to gain access to the children's existing ideas and to make professional decisions as to how they can be developed, modified or changed and the gap closed. For some children this gap exists because of poor preparation for school (Donaldson, 1978). If we wish to close the learning gap, we need to engage in a partnership with children and parents as well as professional colleagues, to plan a teaching and learning pathway that will best meet our educational aims and objectives, the children's needs and abilities and the requirements of the curriculum.

This planning is supported by effective formative assessment to ascertain the children's strengths and targets for development. The introduction of the Foundation Stage Profile (QCA, 2003) provided an opportunity to provide quality summative assessment at the end of the Foundation Stage and gave guidelines for quality formative assessment, which occurred simultaneously with development. However, the bureaucracy and anomalies regarding purpose and practice has failed to influence more widespread practice in Key Stage 1 and it is difficult to see how children move from a skills-based curriculum in the Foundation Stage to a more knowledge-based curriculum in Key Stage 1. Planning development of learning in primary science needs to take into consideration needs and abilities in terms of concepts, knowledge, skills and attitudes. These needs and abilities can be ascertained in a number of ways, as described below, but it is important that practitioners plan for the learning they wish to undertake; that is, they should have clear learning objectives. In the activities on the human body with Reception and Year 1 children described above, the learning objectives (with reference to the Foundation and National Curricula, DfEE, 1999; QCA, 2000) were:

Understandings
- To develop Knowledge and Understanding of the World, identifying the similarities and differences between themselves and others, the external parts of their bodies (KS1 Sc 2) and the main internal organs of the body;
- To develop their vocabulary relating to the human body (arm, leg, head, body, hand, finger, toe, foot and for some children knuckle, knee, wrist, waist, thigh, shin and for a few stomach, brain, lungs, heart). (ELG Language for Communication; KS1 En1)

Skills
- To develop exploratory skills by using all their senses (ELG Exploration and Investigation; KS1 Sc 1) in their observations.
- To develop communication skills and ability to interact with others in communicating. (ELG Language for Communication; KS1 En1)

Attitudes
- To develop cooperative attitudes in the area of Personal, Social and Emotional Development and learn about care and concern for others. (ELG Dispositions and Attitudes)

Clarity of learning objectives will enable the practitioner to both evaluate learning and make individual assessments to support further development. For example, the level of challenge can be evaluated by seeing how the children achieve the objectives. If most children were able to identify names of parts of the body, similarities and differences between themselves and others, then the next activity needs to be more challenging. If most children were identifying similarities and naming some parts of the body, the level of challenge was correct. If most children needed support to identify obvious similarities, the next lesson needs to provide more support and less challenge. Individuals can be assessed using the relevant parts of the Foundation Profile or Key Stage 1 level descriptions. Josh, a reception child, could identify the main differences between him and his friends, pointing out the different colour hair and height (Knowledge and Understanding of the World 4. Identify features of living things and talk about my likes and dislikes). Colin (Year 1) was able to identify similarities and differences and accurately and with detail, label an outline of himself (Sc 2 Level 2).

Planning for the development of scientific skills

Children can be observed while they are exploring and their skills can be noted. Asking questions can help to focus on their skills. For example, if we ask children to tell us about the differences between different objects during a floating and sinking exploration, we can ascertain their observational skills. If they are able to raise questions from their observations, such as 'Do all wooden objects float?' or 'Why do some things seem to float and sink?', we can ascertain their skills in raising questions. Listening to their discussions can tell us if they are able to hypothesize about why some objects float or sink: 'I think all these things will float because they are little.' We can observe children planning investigations and ascertain their ability to plan, make predictions, measure and record data, and we can question them about their investigations or analyse their written work, drawings or any other records. We can also see how they have drawn together their ideas and begun to interpret their data (QCA, 2003).

Planning for the development of scientific skills involves the practitioner in identifying the needs and abilities of the children, deciding how these skills develop, providing opportunities for the development to occur and facilitating that development. In deciding to develop observational skills with young children, practitioners should provide exploratory opportunities for close observation to occur. Children should be encouraged to use their full senses in their observations. The provision of observational aids should assist observation. The children should then be encouraged to notice small details in their observations as well as similarities and differences between things. It may also be appropriate to make sense of observations through classification. The skills of science cannot effectively be developed in isolation and there needs to be meaningful scientific content developed alongside skills (Ausubel, 1963; McClelland, 1983). The relationship between skills, attitudes and concepts, described in Chapters 2 and 4 as spiralling together like a triple helix, should be remembered when planning for teaching and learning, even in the skills-based Foundation Stage curriculum.

Figure 6.1   Formative assessment in the early years; finding out about children

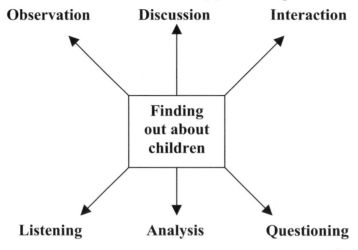

Observation   **Discussion**   **Interaction**

Finding
out about
children

Listening   **Analysis**   **Questioning**

Planning for conceptual development

The importance of eliciting children's existing ideas is widely accepted (e.g. Scott, 1987; de Bóo; Harlen, 2000; QCA, 2003), and becomes more important when we become aware of children's varied ideas and the differing ways these ideas develop. The work of Piaget (1929) did much to advance our knowledge of how children's ideas develop. More recent work by the CLIS 1982–9 and SPACE 1986–90 projects has highlighted some of the common scientific misconceptions that children hold and the way some conceptual development occurs and led to a wealth of smaller but important research which has helped us to understand children's conceptual development. The implications of the research findings are clear. Effective teaching and learning are dependent on children's existing ideas and rely on knowledge of these ideas and subsequent good teaching. We need to ascertain the ideas children hold and the influences on their ideas before we can plan to develop their ideas further, modify their ideas or change them completely. If we are to develop, modify or change children's ideas we need time to find out those ideas and to plan appropriate activities to challenge them. We also need additional time for reflection to enable children to consolidate new or more developed ideas. This is the basis of constructivist learning as outlined by the Children's Learning in Science (CLIS) 1982–9 (Scott, 1987) project; the remodification of any misconceptions and new learning occurs when individual children are allowed to construct their own meaning through experience with the physical environment and through social interaction. This is an active and continuous process whereby children construct links with their prior knowledge, generating new ideas, checking and restructuring old ideas or hypotheses.

The techniques in Figure 6.1 can also be used to find out children's ideas in a particular concept area. Analysis of children's work can include writing, stories and pictures. In each case, discussion about the work is essential to ensure that you understand the child's view of the world. Another useful way to ascertain children's conceptual ideas is to analyse concept maps (Novak and Gowan, 1984), described earlier in Chapter 3. Concept mapping has been found to be a useful tool by teachers to ascertain children's existing ideas, begin the process of introducing a theme and inform planning. Teachers have also used concept mapping to give children more independence in assessing their own knowledge and limitations and to begin to identify their own learning needs. It is important to remember that it is not a tool that will necessarily be successful when first used, as children may need some experience in this way of mapping out their ideas. It would also not be useful to use it on too regular a basis as children may find it tedious. Cross (1992) used pictorial concept maps with young children who found writing difficult. Group concept maps can also be useful, but in order to inform planning to match children's needs and abilities it is most important to listen to the interactions during the mapping and to question children about their emerging ideas. Once children's existing ideas have been ascertained, the practitioner's role involves planning for experiences which will develop, modify or change existing ideas. During planned activities the practitioner should gauge the learning situation and be flexible enough to change plans in order to achieve development. The practitioner also needs to interact with the children and guide their activity so that new ideas can be constructed by them and they have opportunities to reflect on their old ideas and emerging new ideas.

Planning for the development of attitudes

Chapter 4 identified the need to develop children's scientific attitudes. The techniques in Figure 6.1 also apply here. Listening to children engaged in their work will help to identify their attitudes in and to science, as will questioning them and discussing their ideas. Drawing pictures of scientists can also be revealing (Chambers, 1983) but it is essential that children have an opportunity to explain their ideas and pictures. This will enable us to look at science from the children's perspective and prevent us from making assumptions about their attitudes based on our own experiences and views.

Planning for learning styles

Learning preferences are likely to affect and be affected by scientific attitudes, but also by adult preferences (Johnston, 1996) as discussed in Chapter 3, so that practitioners who are very aural learners are likely to prefer to teach more verbally than a practitioner who is more visual or kinaesthetic. Planning should take children's learning preferences into consideration. There are many ways in which we can learn and some of these are listed in Table 6.2. We all have preferred ways of learning. Many children and adults would like to think that learning could be passive and it would be wonderful if knowledge, skills and attitudes could be imparted to us with little or no personal effort. But passive learning is not a reality. We need to be part of the learning process, whatever learning method is used and whatever our learning preference. If we read a book or watch a television programme, learning will not occur unless we participate in some way, and willing, active participation will achieve greater development. We are not always aware that we are participating but it is necessary for learning of any kind to take place. Some learning preferences do appear to need less participation but I would argue that unless we are fully engaged in the concepts, knowledge and skills involved then learning will not be fully effective and may even be impaired. More passive forms of learning are also less likely to develop scientific skills and this is an additional reason in support of active learning. In planning for scientific development we need to plan to widen learning preferences, to enable children to learn in a variety of situations and through a variety of media. For most early-years children, practical experience is essential and cannot be replaced. Secondary sources such as books, television and worksheets can be used to initiate or back up practical learning for older children but cannot replace it.

Table 6.2 Ways of learning in science and about science

Listening to other children
Listening to teachers
Using the computer
Investigating your own ideas
Reading books
Visits to museums, science centres
Watching science television programmes
Following worksheet activities
Discussing ideas with children and teachers
Planning individual projects
Copying from a book, worksheet or the board
Planning work with others in a group

Planning for the learning context

'Excellent teaching gives children the life chances they deserve ... Enjoyment is the birthright of every child. But the most powerful mix is the one that brings the two together' (C. Clark, DfES, 2003: Foreword). Children need excellent teaching and planning for the learning context is one step towards it.

The context of learning is another essential ingredient of an effective early-years classroom. Children require an atmosphere that will nurture learning, allow ideas to be freely expressed and enable failure to develop into success, without any associated fears. As with all aspects of learning, home–school partnership is important (QCA, 2000; Johnston, 2002b). If children find school an alien environment they are less likely to learn. The more prepared children are for school life and the more prepared the teacher is for the child's development the more successful learning will be. Harlen (1977b: 4–5) describes an atmosphere conducive to learning as a helping atmosphere; an atmosphere that encourages in each child enthusiasm for and concern about his or her work; that avoids boredom and frustration; that gives each child security and offers him or her the freedom of choice which is appropriate to their level of development and past experience.

An atmosphere in which children are able to express themselves without their ideas being belittled and where they can be motivated to develop new ideas or expand their ideas would constitute a 'helping atmosphere'. The classroom atmosphere is dependent upon relationships within the school and between school and home. In the classroom the children need to respect the needs of others and the class rules (social and emotional development). This respect should help to establish the classroom atmosphere. Children need to have a relationship with adult practitioners built on trust where they feel able to express their ideas and concerns, and this should extend to their peers. Within the class or school, a helping atmosphere can be developed through shared aims, rules and educational philosophy.

Scientific development will also be assisted if the learning context starts from the familiar and progresses to the unfamiliar. Both practitioner and child feel more confident with familiar phenomena and once both feel secure and are motivated unfamiliar phenomena seem less threatening. Another advantage of using familiar objects and events in science is that it will help to establish the everyday nature of science. Science will then cease to be something that occurs only in the laboratory or classroom and will become something observable in all aspects of life, thus developing knowledge and understanding of the world. Exploring a range of everyday materials or bubbles using different washing-up liquids is less threatening than using prisms, lenses and electrical equipment, although we should not underestimate the motivating force of 'scientific' resources in some situations. Scientific development will also be assisted if the context is cross-curricular and not focused on specific scientific concepts; an approach increasingly becoming more popular after a number of years of decline and which can be highly effective with thorough planning and the identification of clear educational objectives.

Planning for continuity, differentiation and progression

Continuity, differentiation and progression are three closely linked areas which affect teaching and learning. Each has an important part to play in effective child development. Together they illustrate how effective teaching and learning are a result of the close partnership between parents, practitioners, school and child. Practitioners should strive to achieve continuity, differentiation and progression. However, it is also important that continuity, differentiation and progression do not become straitjackets which hinder the provision of good motivating science explorations in which children can differentiate their experiences to meet their own needs and abilities. Reality is often removed to a greater or lesser extent from the ideal and we must be realistic in our expectations, and not despair if our desired aims seem far removed from the reality in our settings. Remember that 'just because something doesn't do what you planned it to do, doesn't mean it's useless' (T. A. Eddison). We have already discussed the importance of continuity within the school. Continuity is the responsibility of the whole school. Shared philosophy, ideas and planning will help to provide continuity of experience. If we plan children's experiences carefully we can ensure that they begin by learning within a familiar context and as they develop, the context becomes more unfamiliar and they have the opportunity to consider how useful their ideas are in a variety of situations. This assists their learning by firming up their ideas. Primary schools, with attached nurseries have the advantage of better liaison between the Foundation Stage, Key Stage 1 and Key Stage 2, usually because of day-to-day contact, and children are often unaware that they are moving between key stages. In separate nurseries, infant and junior schools there needs to be good liaison to ensure that the children's development is not discontinuous. Good liaison will enable young children's exploratory work to be built upon throughout their early experiences. This can be and is a reality in many contexts where 'family planning' takes on a different meaning and a family of schools – that is, secondary schools, their feeder primary schools and nurseries, playgroups, etc. – work together in curriculum areas to ensure some degree of continuity.

Figure 6.2   Planning for continuity, differentiation and progression

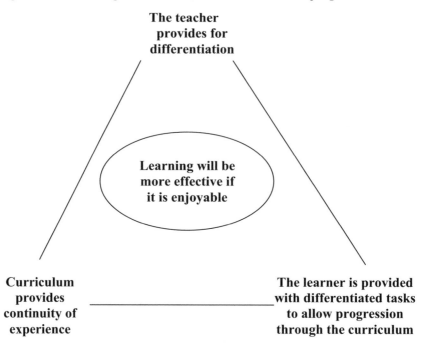

The teacher provides for differentiation

Learning will be more effective if it is enjoyable

Curriculum provides continuity of experience

The learner is provided with differentiated tasks to allow progression through the curriculum

Practitioners are responsible for ensuring that the work they provide matches the needs and abilities of each child. As children are unique, with individual abilities, their developmental and educational needs will differ. Practitioners should provide differentiated activities to meet these differing needs. Children's differentiated needs and abilities can be ascertained in a variety of ways (see Figure 6.1) which can involve practitioners, parents and the child. Parents can provide valuable information about their children. Previous teachers can provide accurate assessments and information about the context of previous work. Children know their own abilities and will add to a developing profile of themselves. The practitioner's role is to collate this information and use it to plan experiences for children which will further their scientific development.

The resulting explorations can be differentiated in a number of ways: by task; by outcome; by starting points; by context and by support. This can be shown through explorations on the theme of sound for Key Stage 1 children. All activities have the same learning aim in terms of the development of the concept of sound. All involve developing knowledge that there are different types of sound and sound sources, that sounds travel from the sound sources to the ear, that some sounds are fainter than others and that when further away from the source, sounds are fainter (Key Stage 1 Sc 4). The children are given a range of objects which make sound in different ways. These can include musical instruments, toys which make a noise, a stop clock, a cassette player with cassette, a ruler, some beads in a jar and some rubber bands.

Explorations that are differentiated by outcome are common and appropriate in science, but it is essential that the practitioner plans what outcome they expect. In the Foundation Stage, it may be expected that most children will be able to identify the objects that make different sounds, although some children may find this difficult and need support. In Year 1 children might be expected to identify differences between the sounds (high, low, loud, quiet), but some more advanced children may be expected to begin to identify how they can change the sound made (make it higher, lower, quieter or louder). In such an exploration, the children are given the objects to explore and after a period of exploration they are asked questions to find out their ideas about sounds and to help them to raise questions for further exploration. Questions can include:

- What do you notice about these objects?
- What do they all do?
- Do they make noises in different ways?
- Which ones are the noisiest/quietest?
- How do you know they are noisy or quiet?
- How can we make this sound quieter/louder?
- How can we hear the sound better?

Individual children will work at their own level and will achieve differentiated learning outcomes according to their ability. Evaluation of the activity will enable practitioners to ascertain how appropriate their planned expectations are for the children.

Explorations on sound that are differentiated by task can take a variety of forms. They are particularly useful in a class with very wide and varying needs and abilities, for example in a vertically grouped class or where some children have special educational needs. Again children are given a range of objects which make sound in different ways. Younger or less able children can be encouraged to explore the objects and then play a sound identification game. This could be in the form of a game in which different sounds have to be described. A child or adult describes or imitates the sound and the children have to guess which object made the sound. Another game could use home-made sound lotto cards with pictures of the objects which are covered when the child hears the noise they make. The winner of the game is the first person to cover all the sounds on their card. Older or more able children could explore the sounds, and place them in order of the things that make loud sounds graduating to the things that make quieter sounds. They can then draw pictures of the objects that make the loudest sounds and the objects that make the quietest sounds. Even older or more able children could explore how to make a loud sound quiet or a quiet sound loud and draw annotated pictures of how the sound reaches their ears and why it is loud or quiet. Differentiation by task also involves considerable teacher planning and organization. Special care is needed in elicitation ability, planning and implementation to ensure that activities are at the correct level of ability and not perceived as of less importance or interest than that of others.

Activities on sound that have differentiated starting points could provide a sequence of explorations of varying difficulty. Children could work through these from different starting points, depending on their needs and abilities. This type of differentiation can have many similarities with differentiation by task, with children moving from the set activity to the next if appropriate. Children who start by exploring sounds and playing identification games could move on to sound sorting, and children beginning with explorations and sorting sounds could move on to exploring how to make sounds quieter or louder. Children who begin by exploring how to make a loud sound quiet or a quiet sound loud could then map out quiet and loud places in the school and undertake some problem-solving to discover where the best place to undertake a loud activity would be. This type of differentiation needs care to avoid starting the child at an inappropriate level and then having to change course.

Differentiation by context takes into account that changes in context from familiar to unfamiliar make the exploration more difficult. Looking at sound within the context of music would be familiar to most children. It could take into consideration favourite music or music of different cultures and use familiar instruments to explore sounds. A more complex context would be looking at sound-proofing, although here there could be familiar or unfamiliar contexts. An exploration which looks at what material makes the best earmuffs for working in a noisy classroom is easier than one which looks at how to sound-proof a noisy clock. The context can be made more difficult by changing the questions you ask the children while they are exploring.

- Which are the quietest earmuffs?
- Which material will make the best earmuffs?
- How can you find out which material will make the best earmuffs?
- Can you find out which material will make earmuffs which are warm and sound-proof?

In each case described above, differentiation by support may also be needed. Flexibility is essential so that additional challenge can be provided for those children who are more able and additional support for those who are struggling to achieve the learning objectives.

Thorough planning is also necessary to provide work that will allow children to progress at their own rate. Practitioners can plan differentiated activities that allow the children to progress at a rate compatible with their individual needs and abilities. This means that teachers need to plan for flexibility and the children need to be active partners in their own development. Progression in learning involves children in developing their own ideas. They need to be able to explore these and construct their own meanings, and this involves an element of flexibility in teaching. Planning is still important but planning should not be so rigid that it hinders progression.

Planning also needs to take into consideration that sequential learning is dependent upon earlier ideas and that learning may involve regression. Remember that there is no single way of developing ideas, and children's learning may not be linear (see Chapter 3). Indeed, it may seem on occasions that children's ideas have regressed when in fact they are more complex ideas. Progressive work should provide greater levels of demand and complexity. It should also aim to meet more complex learning objectives and involve the children in the application of previously acquired ideas, as well as new development or modifications. It is important to note that progression is different from sequencing. A teacher will provide a sequence of activities but individual children will progress through the sequence at their own rate and in their own way. The rate and way of learning are affected by many factors which cannot all be accounted for. Home life, peers, teachers, the type of work set are among factors that can all affect motivation, interest and progression.

Remember that continuity, differentiation and progression cannot be completely prescribed and the most important consideration for teachers is to do your best, relax and enjoy your teaching experiences.

Planning for organization

There are a number of different ways we can organize science activities. In the youngest settings the most important factors are that the organization helps children in their development, linking previous and new experiences, challenges the child and encourages them in their learning as an individual (Hohmann and Weikart, 2002; Riley, 2003).With older children in Key Stage 1 classrooms there can be many effective methods, but planning is needed to ensure that the method best matches the learning aims and objectives, and that children have the opportunity to develop scientific skills along with concepts, knowledge and attitudes. Dean (2001) provides a profile of organizational preferences which can help practitioners to analyse their own style and help decision-making in organization. With each method of organization the practitioner's role will be different. Harlen and Jelly (1997: 37) identify three roles the practitioner can adopt: 'provider of expert knowledge, fellow enquirer and technician'. Changing the teaching role is a useful strategy to help children to engage in different roles within science activities.

The introduction of the Foundation Curriculum (QCA, 2000) has had a positive effect on the organization of explorations in many early-years settings, although national strategies (DfEE, 1998; DfEE, 1999a) have led to less desirable changes which have had an adverse affect on scientific development (ASE, 1999) at Key Stages 1 and 2. Whole-class work can be appropriate for introducing activities, assisting organization, gathering ideas and making sense of ideas. It can also be appropriate for some activities which would be organizationally difficult in small groups, where the children's safety would be difficult to manage and where resource implications make small-group or individual work a problem. I have used whole-class time to introduce animals into the classroom. This can include pets such as rabbits, guinea-pigs, rats, mice and dogs, as well as more unusual animals such as lizards, frogs, snakes and stick insects. The animals can be introduced and emphasis can be placed on the need to be quiet and not to startle or over-handle the animals.

Other introductions and close observations could also take on a similar format. Close observation of a candle flame would be unsafe without careful adult supervision, and while whole-class carpet time would not achieve the same individual observations it would be preferable to no observations at all. Sharing observations in a large group can be beneficial in its own way, as children will have the opportunity to perceive the object from the viewpoints of others. Carpet time can also be used to share ideas after observations and explorations. They can provide the stimulus for new exploratory avenues (Dean, 2001) or help children to make sense of their ideas and interpretations, by using higher-order questioning and opportunities to develop thinking (Kyriacou, 2001). The teacher's role in these sessions changes from motivator to imparter of knowledge to facilitator of learning, depending on the purpose of the activity and the teacher's interactions within the activity. While whole-class teaching is desirable for some aspects of teaching, it does have its problems. The major problem arises because it is impossible to differentiate an activity for whole-class teaching and teaching tends to be planned with the average child in mind and also because young children cannot concentrate for long periods of time – ten minutes being the optimum time for listening activities in the early years.

Small-group work can take a number of different organizational forms (see Hallam *et al.*, 2002). Groups can be organized according to ability, and this would be particularly appropriate with a class of vertically grouped children differentiated by task. It should be remembered that children's abilities in science may not be the same as their abilities in other subjects, and grouping by ability should not be taken to mean grouping by age. Young children develop at a great rate and their abilities in the early years can appear to be very diverse. We often assign them to ability groups based on their maturation, or their language development but we must be aware that they can mature rapidly and that the more articulate is not necessarily the more able scientifically. Ability groupings in the early years should consider the rapid development at this age and not be rigid. Mixed-ability groups, gender groups and friendship groups can all be appropriate in different ways and for different purposes (Dean, 2001). Mixed-ability groups enable the less able to be supported by the more able, mixed and single-sexed groups can have their merits in later years and friendship groups can help motivate children and encourage development, although they can lead to distraction. There is no single 'correct' way to group children. I would suggest that groups are reviewed and changed regularly, so that children become used to working in a variety of situations and with different people. This would be good preparation for future life and aid the development of important group-work and social skills.

Within the classroom, group work can also be organized in different ways. Rotational group work is common in the Foundation Stage, with children in small groups working on similar tasks throughout the day or the week. The advantage of this type of group work is that it is relatively easy to plan and easy on resources. Monitoring explorations and facilitating learning is easier if only one group of children is engaged in practical activity of this nature. Facilitating the learning becomes more difficult if there are a number of very practical activities occurring in the classroom at the same time. The role of the practitioner during the group work is to question and encourage the children to follow lines of enquiry and to monitor their learning and assess their future needs. This group work could, however, be developmental, with each group taking its starting point from the previous group's end point (see Chapter 2). This type of group organization could be very appropriate for ability groups where the children differentiate the activity for the next group according to their outcome and the activity becomes more complex. When the whole class is undertaking science in small groups, it is very demanding on resources, teacher time and sanity, and I have rarely managed it effectively with early-years children. A circus of group activities can be more successful but is equally time-consuming for the practitioner. In this method of organization there are a number of differing science activities, connected to a theme. These are usually structured although they can include some exploratory activities. The activities are set out in the classroom and the children visit each activity during the course of a day or week, being briefed by the teacher at the beginning of each session. I have used this method of organization with Key Stage 2 children where one day per week has been set aside for science work. Within one year group, a science circus has enabled staff to pool expertise and resources and the children to focus on one science activity each week. This is felt (Harlen, 1985) to be of motivational advantage and be relatively easy to organize. I am not convinced about the ease of organization but agree that the main disadvantages of circus activities are the lack of coherence and continuity in the activities and the difficulties of introducing and discussing activities. The 'carpet time' becomes unmanageable.

Individual science work is usually more appropriate for older children, in that it is difficult to organize with young children. However, it can be incorporated into the early years classroom. The use of an interactive science display, science table or play area is one way to encourage individual exploration. This can take the form of a set of resources set out in the classroom which the children can interact with. There may be some simple questions or problems to solve. It may include a 'broken' electrical circuit which the children have to 'mend' or a collection of toys which move in different ways, or a collection of artefacts for close observation, drawing or printing purposes. Books and pictures can be added to encourage the children to look at secondary sources and to motivate them further within the theme. Children like to add to these collections, bringing books and artefacts from home, and this can be a good motivating link with home. I once had a collection of bones in the classroom which were added to by a small boy carrying a plastic bag with a cow's skull inside. 'I found this in a field', he said. 'I thought you would like it.' A kindly mother and a baby bath of bleach soon had the skull presentable for classroom use and it has provided many a stimulus over the years. During a topic on sound a science box was provided with plastic wallets containing ideas for explorations and a simple question. For example, one wallet contained a shaker and the instruction 'Make a sound pattern with the shaker'; it then asked 'Can you think of a way of writing down your pattern?' and gave some examples. Another contained a comb and some greaseproof paper and asked the children to make a noise with them. Using the science table or box idea can be part of the normal early-years day. Children could choose or be directed to the science activities as part of their structured play activities. I have found this to be a good way of motivating the children; it has led to further group and individual work arising from their own interests.

The different methods of organizing science in the classroom are all appropriate for the Key Stage 1 classroom, but not in isolation. A variety

Picture 6.5 *A discovery table*

of organizational approaches is desirable as this will help to widen children's learning preferences and enhance their development.

A questioning approach in action

Planning for the teacher's role, the children's learning, for the context of learning, continuity, differentiation and progression and classroom organization seems like an enormous job. It is a task that we do almost unconsciously. The danger with 'getting on with the job' is that we do not have time to reflect on our practice and assess the children's development, with all the factors affecting it in mind. If we are able to reflect on our practice and ascertain the children's development we should be better informed to make planning decisions, for both our teaching strategies and the children's learning. Next we will consider an exploratory activity from both the teaching and learning viewpoints and see how they develop in practice.

Sarah had a class of 24 Reception and Year 1 children. She planned a topic on minibeasts in conjunction with her school's planning and the requirements of the Foundation Stage Curriculum and the National Curriculum in science. She identified the main areas of learning she wished the children to develop within both the key area of Knowledge and Understanding of the World and Sc 2, Life Processes and Living Things, and Sc 1, Scientific Enquiry. She hoped to develop the following aspects.

(a) Concepts
Variation and classification
Living things in their environment

(b) Knowledge
Minibeasts live in the local environment
Minibeasts can be found in the soil, above the soil, in the air, in plants and trees
There are different minibeasts which can be grouped according to observable features
Minibeasts are adapted to their environment
Minibeasts have needs and we should care for them

(c) Skills
Planning safe collection and study of minibeasts
Observation of minibeasts in their natural environment
Safe collection of minibeasts
Observation of minibeasts in the classroom
Raising questions about minibeasts

(d) Attitudes
Curiosity about the environment
Care for living things.

She particularly wanted to develop her teaching strategies to encourage the children to raise questions. She began to plan activities for the theme which matched her learning aims. The children had no formal experience in this area, but she built into her planning opportunities for them to explore from their own interests using previous knowledge. She considered how she could develop the whole learning environment to encourage children to raise questions. One child's parent kept an allotment and grew vegetables, and the child appeared more knowledgeable about animals in the soil. This parent volunteered to come to school and help during the collection of minibeasts. Sarah collected resources which might be useful for collecting and observing minibeasts (pots, jars, pooters – small pots for collecting insects by sucking them in using two separate tubes, and which allow them to be released afterwards – paintbrushes, spades, trowels, an umbrella and magnifiers). She set up a table in the classroom with books on minibeasts, pictures and the resources for collecting and caring for them.

The introductory activity involved a carpet-time discussion where children were asked to identify any animals they might find in the school garden, field or local environment. Sarah attempted to encourage the children's ideas by allowing each child the opportunity of participating and encouraging the others to listen. She did this by using a 'gardener's hat' which had to be worn before contribution to the discussion. The children were asked to listen attentively to the person with the 'gardener's hat' on and not to speak out of turn. This was followed by discussion on how minibeasts could be carefully found and collected and the places they would most likely be found in. The children were then put into groups and each group had the responsibility of observing a different area. Each group had an adult helper, a classroom assistant and two parents, in addition to the teacher. One group looked for minibeasts in a tree, looking first at the leaves, branches and bark and then using the umbrella to hook over a branch and shake any living things out into the umbrella. Another group looked for minibeasts in the long grass at the edge of the school grounds, while a third group looked at the surface of the soil and a fourth group dug a hole about 20 centimetres into the soil and collected minibeasts from there. All groups were encouraged to note where the minibeasts were found and where possible to observe them before safely collecting them. Some minibeasts were observed in the environment and left, such as a spider in its web on the hedge at the edge of the school field.

In the classroom, the minibeasts were carefully observed, compared and grouped. The children had collected a number of minibeasts including woodlice, snails, earthworms, a beetle, a centipede, greenfly and a hairy caterpillar, as well as evidence of minibeast activity such as eaten leaves and leaf-miner tunnels. Close observation led to drawing, writing, classification using their own criteria (number of legs, shape, where found) and questions being raised about the minibeasts. At the end of the day most of the minibeasts were returned safely to their environment. The earthworms were put into a large plastic sweet jar with layers of damp compost and sand inside and leaf mould was collected and put on the top. The jar was covered with black paper and left on the display table. The woodlice were put into a plastic tub containing damp soil, some leaf mould and some pieces of rotting wood, and the caterpillar was put into a clear container with an assortment of leaves. These were put on the display table along with the books, pictures and resources. The minibeasts were kept in the classroom for a few weeks and observed and cared for by the children. As Sarah wanted to develop the children's ability to raise questions, she used a variety of strategies to encourage this development. She planned questions to focus their observations and develop their questioning skills. For example, she asked each group of children to note all their observations and to share them with the rest of the class during carpet time. During the class discussions she used a white-board to record the questions raised, and she used some of these questions to make question cards to put on the display with the minibeasts.

- Where does it live?
- How many legs?
- What can you see?
- What does it eat?

She then asked the children to identify which questions they could begin to answer from their observations. The children used their observations to keep individual records of the minibeasts and tried to answer the questions. Leanne chose to keep a record of the caterpillar. She was interested in the caterpillar's food, having been motivated by the story of *The Very Hungry Caterpillar* (Carle, 1970). The caterpillar ate a great deal of leaves, although not lollipops, Swiss cheese or ice cream, and then stopped eating. Leanne predicted that the caterpillar would turn into a butterfly quickly, but it seemed to take a long time. She was puzzled but kept watching. When the minibeast topic was complete and the other minibeasts returned to their natural environment, the chrysalis was kept in the classroom and Leanne, along with other children, kept a close watch on it. When it eventually turned into a moth, Leanne was delighted and finished the last page of her 'caterpillar diary'. An extended study had resulted from a small hairy caterpillar found in the school grounds. The moth was released into the playground and the children watched it fly away.

Table 6.3　Roles and experience in a topic on minibeasts

Teacher's role	Children's experience
Researcher and planner	
Motivator	Whole-class introduction to topic
Instructor	Whole-class instruction in collecting and caring for minibeasts
Guide	Group observation and collection of minibeasts
Interactor	Small-group observations and question raising
Convener	Small-group and whole-class discussions
Motivator	Adding to interactive display
Guide and interactor	Small-group and individual recording of minibeasts

During this work there were a number of different teaching roles and learning experiences. These are listed in Table 6.3. During the teaching and learning, Sarah observed the children and made assessments of their learning in line with her main learning aims. In some cases she adjusted teaching and learning demands according to the needs of individual children. One group of reception children found group interaction difficult. Sarah gave each child the task of observing and writing about one minibeast and compiling a group book about the minibeasts. The children had to decide which minibeast they wished to observe and plan their book before they could work individually. They needed help in putting the book together, but they made some attempt at developing group-work skills.

After each stage of the teaching it was necessary for Sarah to reflect on her teaching and the children's learning and to be flexible enough to modify her planning to meet her learning aims, or modify her learning aims to meet the needs of the children. Good planning was necessary, but not inflexibility.

I hope that all teachers would have not only the ability, but also a willingness, to reflect on their own practice. Teacher education, both initial training and in-service, should involve elements of classroom action research. Classroom action research on initial teacher training courses is felt to be extremely valuable by both students and educationists (Elliott, 1991; Frost, 1997), and I see student teachers entering the teaching profession having researched children's learning and their own practice, and with a clear idea of their teaching role. The skills developed as a result benefit both the children's learning and the teaching strategies to aid that learning.

Summary

- The practitioner's role is varied and complex.
- Practitioners need to plan carefully not only for the children's learning but for their own role to facilitate that learning.
- Effective practitioners of young children are also reflective.
- For young children the most effective roles involve the practitioner as a facilitator of learning rather than an imparter of knowledge.

References

Ager, R. (2000) *The Art of Information and Communication Technology for Teachers.* London: David Fulton.

Ahtee, M. and Johnston, J. (2005) Primary student teachers' ideas about teaching a physics topic. *Scandinavian Journal of Science Education* (awaiting publication).

Ahlberg, A. (1981) *Mrs Lather's Laundry.* London: Penguin (Picture Puffin).

Ahlberg, J. and Ahlberg, A. (1980) *Funnybones.* London: Collins Picture Lions.

Aikenhead, G. (2000) Renegotiating the Culture of School Science. In R. Millar, J. Leach and J. Osborne (eds) *Improving Science Education: The contribution of research.* Buckingham: Open University Press.

Allen, P. (1986) *Mr Archimedes Bath.* London: Hamish Hamilton.

Anning, A. (1991) *The First Years at School.* Buckingham: Open University Press.

Antonouris, G. (1991) Teaching science in a multicultural society. *Primary Science Review*, 17: 3–7.

ASE (1993) *The Whole Curriculum in Primary Schools – Maintaining Quality in the Teaching of Primary Science.* Hatfield: ASE.

ASE (1999) *ASE Survey on the Effect of the National Literacy Strategy on the Teaching of Science.* Hatfield: ASE.

ASE (2004) *Primary Science Review. Creativity and Science Education* No. 81 Jan/Feb 2004.

Ausubel, D. P. (1963) *The Psychology of Meaningful Verbal Learning.* New York: Grune & Stratton.

Ausubel, D. (1968) *Educational Psychology: A Cognitive View.* New York: Holt, Rinehart & Winston.

Barnes, D. (1976) *From Communication to Curriculum*. Harmondsworth: Penguin.

Beetlestone, F. (1998) *Creative Children, Imaginative Teaching*. Buckingham: Open University Press.

Bennett, N., Wood, L. and Rogers, S. (1997) *Teaching Through Play: Teachers' Thinking and Classroom Practice*. Buckingham: Open University Press.

BERA (2003) *Early Years Research: Pedagogy, Curriculum and Adult Roles, Training and Professionalism*. Southwell, Notts: BERA.

Berk, L. E. (2003) *Child Development*. 6th edn, Boston, Mass: Allyn & Bacon.

Bliss, J., Mellar, H., Ogborn, J. and Nash, C. (1992) *Tools for Exploratory Learning Programme End of Award Report: Technical Report 2. Semi Quantitative Reasoning-Expressive*. London: University of London.

Boden, M. A. (2001) Creativity and knowledge. In A. Craft, B. Jeffrey and M. Leibling (eds) *Creativity in Education*. London: Continuum.

Bowell, B., France, S. and Redfern, S. (1994) *Portable Computers in Action*. Coventry: National Council for Educational Technology.

Bowlby, J. (1969) *Attachment and Loss*. New York: Basic Books.

Bricheno, P., Johnston, J. and Sears, J. (2000) Children's attitudes to science. In J. Sears and P. Sorensen (eds) *Issues in the Teaching of Science*. London: Routledge.

Briggs, R. (1970) *Jim and the Beanstalk*. London: Penguin (Picture Puffin).

Browne, E. (1997) *Handa's Surprise*. London: Walker Books.

Brown, A. L., Campione, J. C., Metz, K. E. and Ash, D. B. (1997) The development of science learning abilities in children. In K. Härnquist and A. Burgen, *Growing Up with Science: Developing Early Understanding*. London: J. Kingsley.

Bruner, J. S., Goodnow, J. J. and Austin, G. A. (1956) *A Study of Thinking*. New York: Wiley 72(26): 47–63.

Bruner, J. S., Jolly, A. and Sylva, K. (1976) *Play: Its Role in Development and Education*. Harmondsworth, Middx: Penguin.

Carle, E. (1970) *The Very Hungry Caterpillar*. Harmondsworth: Penguin.

Carle, E. (1987) *The Tiny Seed*. London: Hodder and Stoughton.

Catsambis, S. (1995) Gender, race, ethnicity and science education in the middle grades. *Journal of Research in Science Teaching*, 32: 243–57.

Chambers, D. W. (1983) Stereotypic images of the scientist. *Science Education*, 62: 225–65.

Chapman, B. (1991) The overselling of science in the eighties. *Schools Science Review*, 72(26): 47–63.

Childs, D. (1986) *Psychology and the Teacher*. 4th edn, Chatham: Holt, Rinehart & Winston.

Compton, A. (2002) Creative music. In J. Johnston, M. Chater and D. Bell (eds) *Teaching the Primary Curriculum*. Buckingham: Open University Press.

Cook, D. and Finlayson, H. (1999) *Interactive Children, Communicative Teaching: ICT and Classroom Teaching*. Buckingham: Open University Press.

Cosgrove, M. and Osborne, R. (1985) Lesson frameworks for changing children's ideas. In R. Osborne and P. Freyberg, *Learning in Science: The Implications of Children's Learning*. Auckland, New Zealand: Heinemann.

Costello, P. J. M. (2000) *Thinking Skills and Early childhood Education*. London: David Fulton.

Craft, A. (2002) *Creativity and Early Years Education. A lifeworld Foundation*. London: Continuum.

Cross, A. (1992) Pictorial concept maps – putting us in the picture. *Primary Science Review*, 21: 26–8.

Cullingford, C. (1997) Changes in Primary Education. In Cullingford, C. (1996) *The Politics of Primary Education*. Buckingham: Open University Press.

Cumming, J. (1995) An Easter science and technology project involving parents. *Primary Science Review*, 36: 4–7.

Dale Tunnicliffe, S. and Litson, S. (2002) Observation or Imagination? *Primary Science Review*, 71: 25–7.

Dean, J. (2001) *Organising Learning in the Primary Classroom*. 3rd edn, London: Routledge/Falmer.

de Bono, E. (1992) *Serious Creativity*. London: Harper Collins.

de Bóo, M. (1999) *Enquiring Children: Challenging Teaching*. Buckingham: Open University Press.

de Bóo, M. (ed.) (2004) *Early Years Handbook. Support for Practitioners in the Foundation Stage*. Sheffield: The Curriculum Partnership/Geography Association.

De Jong, O. (2003) Exploring Science Teachers' Pedagogical Content Knowledge. In D. Psillos, P. Kariotoglou, V. Tselfes, E. Hatzikraniotis, G. Fassoulopoulos and M. Kallery (eds) *Science Education Research in the Knowledge-Based Society*. Dordrecht: Kluwer Academic Publishers.

Dennison, P. and Dennison, G. (1994) *Brain Gym*. CA: The Educational Kinesiology Foundation.

DES (1967) *Children and their Primary school. A Report of the Central Advisory Council for Education (England) Vol. 1: Report*. London: HMSO.

DES (1987) *National Curriculum Science Working Group. Interim Report*. London: DES.

DES (1988) *A Report: National Task Group on Assessment and Testing*. London: DES.

Dewey, J. (1916) *Democracy and Education. An Introduction to the Philosophy of Education* (1966 edn), New York: Free Press.

DfEE (1998) *The National Literacy Strategy*. London: DFEE.

DfEE (1999) *The National Curriculum: Handbook for Teachers in England*. London: DfEE/QCA.

DfEE (1999a) *The National Numeracy Strategy*. London: DFEE.

DfES (2003) *Excellence and Enjoyment. A strategy for Primary Schools*. London: DfES.

Doherty, J. and Dawe, J. (1988) The relationship between development maturity and attitude to school science. *Educational Studies*, 11: 93–107.

Donaldson, M. (1978) *Children's Minds*. London: Fontana.

Driver, R. (1983) *The Pupil as a Scientist*. Milton Keynes: Open University Press.

Driver, R., Guesne, E. and Tiberghien, A. (eds) (1985) *Children's Ideas in Science*. Milton Keynes: Open University Press.

Duffy, B. (1998) *Supporting Creativity and Imagination in the Early Years.* Buckingham: Open University Press.

Elliott, J. (1991) *Action Research for Educational Change.* Milton Keynes: Open University Press.

Elstgeest, J., Harlen, W. and Symington, D. (1985) Children communicate. In W. Harlen (ed.) *Primary Science: Taking the Plunge.* London: Heinemann.

Erikson, E. H. (1950) *Childhood and Society.* New York: Norton.

Erikson, G. L. (1979) Children's conceptions of heat and temperature. *Science Education*, 63: 221–30.

Evans, S. (2002) Acceleration: A legitimate means of meeting the needs of gifted children. *www.nexus.edu.au.teachstud/gat/evanss.htm*

Faire, J. and Cosgrove, M. (1988) *Teaching Primary Science.* Hamilton, New Zealand: Waikato Education Centre.

Feasey, R. (2003) Creative futures. *Primary Science Review* 78 May/ June 2003: 21–3.

Fensham, P. J. (2001) Science content as problematic – issues for research. In H. Behrendt, H. Dahncke, R. Duit, W. Gräber, M. Komorek, A. Kross and P. Reiska. *Research in Science – Past, Present and Future.* AA Dordrecht, The Netherlands: Kluwer.

Field, T. (1991) Quality infant daycare and grade school behaviour and performance. *Child Development*, 62: 863–70.

Fisher, R. (2003) *Teaching Thinking.* London: Continuum.

Fraser, B. (1981) *Test of Science Related Attitudes: Handbook.* Victoria, Australia: Council for Educational Research.

Fraser, B. and Tobin, K. (1993) Exemplary science and mathematics teachers. In B. Fraser (ed.) *Research Implications for Science and Mathematics Teachers, Volume 1.* Perth, WA: National Key Centre for School Science and Mathematics, Curtin University of Technology.

Fröbel, F. (1826) *On the Education of Man (Die Menschenerziehung).* Keilhau/ Leipzig: Wienbrach.

Frost, D. (1997) *Reflective Action Planning For Teachers: A Guide To Teacher-Led School Development.* London: David Fulton.

Gardner, H. (1983) *Frames of Mind: The Theory of Multiple Intelligences.* London: Heinemann.

Gardner, H. (1991) *The Unschooled Mind.* London: Fontana.

Ginn, I. S. and Watters, J. (1995) An analysis of scientific understanding of preservice elementary teacher education students. *Journal of Research in Science Teaching*, 32 (2): 205–22.

Gold, K. (1990) Get thee to a laboratory. *New Scientist*, 126(1712): 42–6.

Goldsworthy, A. and Feasey, R. (1997) *Making Sense of Primary Investigations.* Revised Edition revised by S. Ball. Hatfield: Association for Science Education.

Green, M. (1978) *Mr Bembleman's Bakery.* New York: Parents Magazine Press.

Haladyna, T., Olsen, R., and Shaunessy, J. (1982) Relations of student, teacher and learning environment variables to attitudes to science. *Science Education*, 66: 671–87.

Hallam, S., Ireson, J. and Davies, J. (2002) *Effective Grouping in the Primary School: A Practical Guide.* London: David Fulton.

Harlen, W. (ed.) (1977a) *Match and Mismatch: Raising Questions.* Edinburgh: Oliver & Boyd.

Harlen, W. (ed.) (1977b) *Match and Mismatch: Finding Answers.* Edinburgh: Oliver & Boyd.

Harlen, W. (1985) *Teaching and Learning Primary Science.* London: Paul Chapman.

Harlen, W. (1992) *The Teaching of Science: Studies in Primary Education.* London: David Fulton.

Harlen, W. (2000) *The Teaching of Science in Primary Schools.* 3rd edn, London: David Fulton.

Harlen, W. (2000a) *Teaching, Learning and Assessing Science 5–12.* 3rd edn, London: Paul Chapman.

Harlen, W. and Holroyd, C. (1997) Primary teachers' understanding of concepts of science: impact on confidence and teaching. *International Journal of Science Education,* 19: 93–105.

Harlen, W. and Jelly, S. (1997) *Developing Science in the Primary Classroom.* Harlow: Longman.

Head, J. (1996) Gender identity and cognitive style. In P. Murphy and C. Gippa (eds) *Equity in the Classroom: Towards Effective Pedagogy for Girls and Boys.* London: Falmer Press/UNESCO.

Hendley, D., Parkinson, J., Stables, A. and Tanner, H. (1995) Gender differences in pupil attitudes to the National Curriculum foundation subjects of English, mathematics, science and technology in Key Stage 3 in South Wales. *Educational Studies,* 21: 85–97.

Hidi, S. and Harackiewicz, J. M. (2000) Motivating the academically unmotivated: a critical issue for the twenty-first century. *Review Of Educational Research* 70 (2): 151–79.

Hohmann, M. and Weikart, D. P. (2002) *Educating Young Children.* 2nd edn, Ypsilanti, Michigan: High/Scope Press.

Intel (2001) *Intel Play QX3.* And Neo/Science Corporation.

Irwin, A. and Wynne, B. (eds) (1996) *Misunderstanding Science? The Public Reconstruction of Science and Technology.* Cambridge: Cambridge University Press.

Isaacs, S. (1930) *Intellectual Growth in Young Children.* London: Routledge.

Jarvis, T. (1994) Schools-based tasks in science for primary postgraduate initial teacher trainees. Paper presented to the Conference for the Australian Science Teachers Association (CONASTA) conference.

Jenkins, E. (2000) Science for all: time for a paradigm shift? In R. Millar, J. Leach and J. Osborne (eds) *Improving Science Education. The Contribution of Research.* Buckingham: Open University Press.

Johnston, C. (1996) *Unlocking the Will to Learn.* California: Corwin Press Inc.

Johnston, J. (1992) The science straitjacket. *Primary Science Review,* 25: 8–9.

Johnston, J. (1998) Learning science in the early years. In R. Sherrington (ed.) *ASE Guide to Primary Science Education.* Cheltenham: Stanley Thornes.

Johnston, J. (2001) Supplement on Observation. *Early Years Educator,* July 2001.

Johnston, J. (2002) The changing face of teaching and learning. In J. Johnston, M. Chater and D. Bell (eds) *Teaching the Primary Curriculum*. Buckingham: Open University Press.

Johnston, J. (2002a) Supplement on making sense of the world. *Early Years Educator*, June 2002.

Johnston, J. (2002b) Teaching and learning in the early years. In J. Johnston, M. Chater and D. Bell (eds) *Teaching the Primary Curriculum*. Buckingham: Open University Press.

Johnston, J. (2003) The importance of language in scientific understanding. *Education Today*, 53 (3): 42–4.

Johnston, J. (2004) The value of exploration and discovery. *Primary Science Review*, 85: 21–3.

Johnston, J., Ahtee, M. and Hayes, M. (1998) Elementary teachers' perceptions of science and science teaching: Comparisons between Finland and England. In S. Kaartinen (ed.) *Matemaattisten Aineiden Opetus ja Oppiminen* (Oulu, Oulun yliopistopaino): 13–30.

Johnston, J. and Ahtee, M. (2005) What are primary student teachers' attitudes, subject knowledge and pedagogical content knowledge needs in a physics topic? *Teaching and Teacher Education* (awaiting publication).

Johnston, J. and Gray, A. (1999) *Enriching Early Scientific Learning*. Buckingham: Open University Press.

Johnston, J. and Herridge, D. (2004) *Heinemann Explore Science, Reception*. Oxford: Heinemann Educational.

Jones, C. (2000) The role of language in the learning and teaching of science. In M. Monk and J. Osborne (eds) *Good Practice in Science Teaching: What Research Has to Say*. Buckingham: Open University Press.

Kahn, P. H. Jr. (1999) *The Human Relationship with Nature*. Cambridge, MA: MIT Press.

Karplus, R. (1977) *Science Teaching and the Development of Reasoning*. Berkeley, CA: University of California Press.

Keogh, B. and Naylor, S. (2000) Assessment in the early years. In de Bóo, M. (ed.) *Laying the Foundations in the Early Years*. ASE: Hatfield.

Keogh, B. and Naylor, S. (2003) 'Do do as I do'; being a role model in the early years. *Primary Science Review*. No. 78.

King, C. (1963) *Stig of the Dump*. Harmondsworth: Penguin.

Kohlberg, L. (1976) Moral stages and moralization: The cognitive-developmental approach. In T. Lickona (ed.) *Moral Development and Behaviour: Theory, Research and Social Issues*. New York: Holt: 31–53.

Kyriacou, C. (2001) *Essential Teaching Skills*. 2nd edn, Cheltenham: Nelson Thornes.

Lindon, J. (2001) *Understanding Children's Play*. Cheltenham: Nelson Thornes.

Maslow, A. H. (1968) *Towards a Psychology of Being*. New York: D. Van Nostrand Co.

Matthews, B. (1996) Drawing scientists. *Gender and Education*, 8 (2): 231–43.

May, S. (1985) *Planet of the Monsters*. London: Picture Corgi.

McClelland, G. (1983) Ausubel's theory of meaningful learning and its implications for primary science. In C. Richards and D. Holford (eds) *The Teaching of Primary Science: Policy and Practice.* Lewes: Falmer Press.

McMillan, M. (1911) *The Child and the State.* Manchester: National Labour Press.

McMillan, M. (1930) *The Nursery School.* London: Dent.

Medawar, P. B. (1969) *Induction and Intuition in Scientific Thought.* Memoirs of the American Philosophical Society. Jayne Lectures 1968. London: Methuen.

Miller, J. D., Pardo, R. and Niwa, E. (1997) *Public Perceptions of Science and Technology: A Comparative Study of the European Union, the United States, Japan and Canada.* Madrid: BBV Foundation.

Millar, R. and Wynne, B. (1988) Public understanding of science. *International Journal of Science Education,* 10: 388–98.

Moyles, J. R. (1989) *Just Playing? The Role and Status of Play in Early Childhood Education.* Buckingham: Open University Press.

Moyles, J. R. (ed.) (1994) *The Excellence of Play.* Buckingham: Open University Press.

Moyles, J. R. and Adams, S. (2001) *StEPS Statements of Entitlement to Play. A Framework for Playful Teaching with 3-7 Year-olds.* Buckingham: Open University Press.

Moyles, J. R., Adams, S., Musgrove, A. (2002) *Study of Pedagogical Effectiveness in Early Learning.* London: DfES.

Munn, N. (1966) *Psychology.* 5th edn, London: Harrap.

Novak, J. and Gowan, D. B. (1984) *Learning How to Learn.* Cambridge: Cambridge University Press.

Ofsted (2003) *The Education of Six Year Olds in England, Denmark and Finland.* London: HMI.

Osborne, R. and Freyberg, P. (1985) *Learning in Science: The Implications of Children's Learning.* Auckland, New Zealand: Heinemann.

Osborne, J., Wadsworth, P. and Black, P. (1992) *Materials,* Primary Science Processes and Concept Exploration (SPACE) project research report. Liverpool: Liverpool University Press.

Ovens, P. (1987) Ice balloons. *Primary Science Review,* 3: 5–6.

Owens, P. (2004) A Basket of Fruit from Kenya. In M. de Bóo, (ed.) *Early Years Handbook. Support for Practitioners in the Foundation Stage.* Sheffield: The Curriculum Partnership/ Geography Association: 80–87.

Piaget, J. (1929) *The Child's Conception of the World.* New York: Harcourt.

Piaget, J. (1950) *The Psychology of Intelligence.* London: Routledge & Kegan Paul.

Prentice, R. (2000) Creativity: a reaffirmation of its place in early childhood education. *The Curriculum Journal,* 11 (2): 145–58.

QCA (2000) *Curriculum Guidance for the Foundation Stage.* London: DFEE.

QCA (2000a) *A Scheme of Work for Key Stages 1 and 2 – Science.* London: QCA.

QCA (2003) *Foundation Stage Profile.* London: QCA.

QCA (2003a) *Creativity: Find It Promote It.* London: QCA/DFEE.

Raper, G. and Stringer, J. (1987) *Encouraging Primary Science.* London: Cassell.

Reiss, M. J. (1993) *Science Education for a Pluralist Society. Developing Science and Technology Education.* Buckingham: Open University Press.

Renner, J. (1982) The power of purpose. *Science Education,* 66: 709–16.

Riley, J. (ed.) (2003) *Learning in the Early Years. A Guide for Teachers of Children 3–7.* London: Paul Chapman.

Ross, C. and Browne, N. (1993) *Girls as Constructors in the Early Years.* London: Trentham Books.

Rousseau, J. J. (1911) *Emile.* London: J. M. Dent and Sons.

Rowland, R. (1981) How to intervene: clues from the work of a ten year old. *Forum,* 23 (2): 33–5.

Rowland, R. (1984) *The Enquiring Classroom: An Approach to Understanding Children's Learning.* London: Falmer Press.

Rowling, J. K. (1997) *Harry Potter and the Philosopher's Stone.* London: Bloomsbury.

Scott, P.(1987) *A Constructivist View of Teaching and Learning Science.* Leeds: Leeds University.

Sears, J. (1995) The Introduction of Balanced Science and Pupil Attitudes. *British Journal of Curriculum and Assessment,* 5 (2): 366–70.

Simon, S. (2000) Students' attitudes towards science. In M. Monk and J. Osborne (eds) *Good Practice in Science Teaching. What Research Has to Say.* Buckingham: Open University Press.

Siraj-Blatchford, I., Sylva, K., Muttock, S., Gilden, R. and Bell, D. (2002) *Researching Effective Pedagogy in the Early Years.* London: DfES.

Siraj-Blatchford, J. (2000) Promoting Equality and Citizenship. In de Bóo (ed.) *Science 3–6 Laying the Foundations in the Early Years.* Hatfield: ASE.

Smail, B. (1984) *Girl-Friendly Science: Avoiding Sex Bias in the Curriculum.* York: Schools Council/Longman.

Spearman, C. (1927) *Abilities of Man.* Basingstoke: Macmillan.

Steiner, R. (1996) *The Education of the Child and Early Lectures on Education.* New York: Anthroposophic Press.

Strauss, S. (1981) *U-shaped Behavioural Growth.* Academic Press.

Sukhnandan, L., Lee, B. and Kelleher, S. (2000) *An Investigation into Gender Differences in Achievement. Phase 2: School and Classroom Strategies.* Slough, Berks: NFER.

Thurstone, L. L. and Thurstone, T. G. (1941) Factorial Studies of Intelligence. *Psychometric Monographs* No. 2.

Tinklin, T. (2003) 'Gender Differences and High Attainment'. *British Educational Research Journal,* 29 (3): 307–25.

Trumper, R. (2003) The need for change in elementary school teacher training: A cross-college age study of future teachers' conceptions of basic astronomy concepts. *Teaching And Teacher Education,* 19: 309–23.

Vygotsky, L. (1962) *Thought and Language.* Cambridge, MA: MIT Press.

Vygotsky, L. and Cole, M. (ed.) (1978) *Mind in Society, The Development of Higher Psychological Proceses.* Cambridge, Mass: Harvard University Press.

Wallace, F. (1994) *Balanced Science Survey.* Hatfield: ASE.

Watt, D. and Russell, T. (1990) *PRIMARY SPACE Sound.* Liverpool: Liverpool University Press.

Wilde, O. (1978) *The Selfish Giant.* London: Penguin (Picture Puffin).

Williams, J. E. and Best, D. L. (1990) *Measuring Sex Stereotypes: A Multination Study.* Newbury Park Ca: Sage.

Woolnough, B. (1994) *Effective Science Teaching*. Buckingham: Open University Press.

Wolfendale, S., Penn, H., Griffiths, F. and Walker, S. (2000) *Special Needs in the Early Years: Snapshots of Practice*. London: Routledge Falmer.

Yager, R. E. and Penick, J. E. (1986) Perceptions of four age groups towards science classes, teachers and the value of science. *Science Education*, 70 (4): 355–63.

Index